KENT & EAST SUSSEX WATERWAYS

P.A.L. VINE

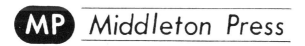

Middleton Press

1989

Waterway	From	To	Year available for commericial use	Distance (nearest mile)	No. of Locks	Year Regular Commercial Traffic Ceased	If Navigable in 1989
Brede	Rye	Brede	Always (tidal until 1786)	8	1	c 1935	Yes
Cuckmere	Cuckmere Haven	Alfriston	c 1770	6	None	1915	Yes
Dartford & Crayford	The Thames	Dartford Crayford	Always (tidal until 1844)	2	1	1987 Open	Partially Yes
Glynde Reach	Beddingham	Glynde	1767	2	None	1928	Small boats
Medway (Lower)	Sheerness	Aylesford Maidstone	Always Always (tidal until 1792)	27	1	Open 1977	Yes
Medway (Upper)	Maidstone	Tovil Tonbridge	1741 1741	16	11 14 (until 1915)	1977 1927	Yes
Ouse (Lower)	Newhaven	Lewes	Always	8	None	1927	Yes
Ouse (Upper)	Lewes	Sheffield Bridge Freshfield Bridge Lindfield Upper Ryelands Br.	1793 1805 1809 1812	22	18	1868 1868 1868 1861	Canoes only
Reading Sewer	Blackwall Bridge	Smallhythe	c 1750	3	None	c 1930	Canoes only
Rother	Rye	Newenden Bodiam	Always (tidal until 1736)	16	1	1933 c1925	Yes
Royal Military Canal - (Sussex) (Kent)	Cliff End Iden	Winchelsea Appledore Hythe Shorncliffe	Never 1810 1810 1810	3 19	None 1	- 1909 c 1880 c 1840	No Small boats
Seaton	Stourmouth	Seaton	1801	6	None	1860	Canoes only
Stour	Pegwell Bay	Fordwich	Always	19	None	c1884	Yes
Thames & Medway Canal	Gravesend	Higham Strood	1824 1824	7	2	1934 1845	No
Tillingham	Rye	Marley Farm	Always (tidal until 1786)	2	1	1928	Canoes only

Design - Deborah Goodridge

Laser typesetting - Barbara Mitchell

First published November 1989

ISBN 0 906520 72 X

Copyright - P. A. L. Vine 1989

Published by Middleton Press
Easebourne Lane
Midhurst, West Sussex
GU29 9AZ
Tel. (0730) 813169

Printed & bound by Biddles Ltd,
Guildford and Kings Lynn

CONTENTS

MAPS

The scale of the Ordnance Survey maps is given in the captions only when it is other than 25" to 1 mile.

ACKNOWLEDGEMENTS

I am very grateful indeed to those who have kindly assisted me or have lent me photographs, and in particular to Ean Begg, Michael Bouquet, Miss Kay Bowen, Brede Women's Institute, John Brown, Canterbury Public Library, Michael Cardew, Miss B. Catt, John Collard, Leonard Coombs, Hugh Compton, The Daily Telegraph, Dartford Central Library, Bob Dawes, Dendy Easton, East Sussex County Record Office, John Farrant, A. J. Franklin, Gravesend Library, Charles Hadfield, Hastings Public Library, Andrew Lusted, Hugh McKnight, Maidstone County Library, Vic Mitchell, Railway & Canal Historical Society, Tom Reeves, Guildhall Museum Rochester, Dr Roger Sellman, Miss F Stringer, Sussex Archaeological Society and Miss Edwina Vine. I would also like to thank the Sunday Times for permission to use photographs from the Edward Reeves Collection.

HISTORICAL BACKGROUND

For centuries, the River Thames and the Port of London formed the vital artery of Britain's commerce. The Thames was never made navigable for it had always been so, although above its tidal reaches, boats were much impeded by fish dams and mill weirs into which were incorporated flash locks. Not, however, until 1635 was the river considered navigable for barges as far as Oxford.

Although the Thames forms the northern boundary of Kent, this book concentrates on the county's waterways which were made navigable or which were used by barges on their tidal reaches. By far the most important was the River Medway whose commercial utility spanned three centuries and played an important role in the development of trade to Maidstone and Tonbridge. However, many of the smaller Kent and Sussex rivers were of considerable utility during the nineteenth century in providing outlets for timber and agricultural produce, while enabling coal and manufactured goods to be imported.

In spite of many proposals for new waterways during the canal era, only three were constructed. Two of these were built by the Government during the Napoleonic Wars - the Royal Arsenal Canal at Woolwich, which was begun in 1812 and completed in 1817, and the Royal Military Canal which was dug 22 miles around Romney Marsh during the Napoleonic Wars, to hinder an invasion force making a landing along the flat part of the Kent coast between Shorncliffe and Winchelsea. The third, and the only canal intended for commerce, was the Thames & Medway Canal whose short existence (1824 - 1845) was terminated by its purchase and partial closure by the Gravesend & Rochester Railway Company.

There were two great canal projects which never came to fruition. The first was John Rennie's Grand Southern Canal which was planned to run from the Medway at Tonbridge to Portsmouth. Its 95 mile line would have passed through Edenbridge, Horsham and Pulborough, with branches to the Adur, Ouse, Croydon Canal and Weald of Kent Canal. Its bill was considered in Parliament but lost

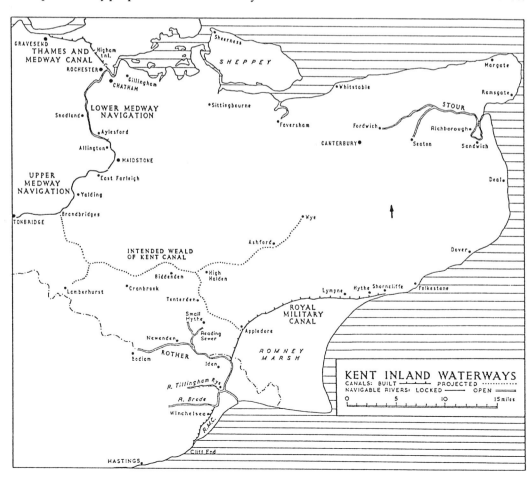

KENT INLAND WATERWAYS
CANALS: BUILT ———— PROJECTED ··········
NAVIGABLE RIVERS: LOCKED ———— OPEN ════
0   5   10   15 miles

on second reading in 1810 by 100 votes to 17. The second was the Weald of Kent Canal which was planned from the River Medway at Brandbridges to the Royal Military Canal at Appledore, a distance of 30 miles with 24 locks. Its Act of Parliament, obtained in 1812, authorised a capital of £305,800 which had to be raised within 3 years before work could start. By 1815 only £103,900 had been subscribed and the attempt was dropped.

Several efforts were also made to provide a waterway to Canterbury, either by building a canal from the sea at St. Nicholas Bay or by improving the River Stour.

The Royal Arsenal Canal at Woolwich was the brainchild of Lt Col Pilkington, Commanding Royal Engineer. During 1810 he initially conceived of the canal as a method of preventing unauthorised people from crossing the eastern boundary of the arsenal. In July 1810 he wrote to Lt Gen Morse, Inspector General of Fortifications, outlining his plan and estimating that it would cost £1,338 for a 45 ft-wide lockless canal with a depth of ten feet to allow cargo vessels to bring timber into the arsenal. After approval had been obtained from both the military authorities and the Commissioners of Sewers, work was begun in 1812. By 1814, William Bough, the contractor, had nearly finished the main line of the canal, but it was found necessary to build an entrance lock and other ancillary works which were not completed until 1817. The total cost was £15,000.

Initial opinion as to the utility of the canal was enthusiastic, but declined after the first few years and although the channel was dredged from time to time, it was not greatly used. The upper part of the canal was filled in over the period between 1926 and 1936 and the remainder was obliterated with the closing of the arsenal and the development of Thamesmead in the mid-1970s. There is therefore scant photographic evidence of this venture.

What is there to see today?

It is still possible to explore the remains of disused locks and grass-grown wharves abandoned over a century ago and to find that they have remained in their original settings, little changed by the passing of the years. Although the current passion of both local and water authorities to tidy up the nooks and crannies of our abandoned waterways has obliterated some of the artificial cuttings and disused buildings which were made to assist waterborne trade, the countryside explorer will find the Sussex Ouse of particular interest when attempting to locate the remains of a navigation which ceased to be used more than a century ago.

I have tried in many cases to show similar views recorded at different periods in the past rather than the present. The town quays, deserted by sailing barges and horses and carts, are now occupied by pleasure craft and motor vehicles. Bridges too have suffered from demolition or have been widened, but there are still fine examples to be seen on the Medway and on the Stour, at Sandwich. The channel of the Royal Military Canal is in good condition but the bed of the Thames & Medway Canal remains in a sorry state.

When investigating the sites of abandoned waterways please check to see if there is a public right of way or request permission to investigate.

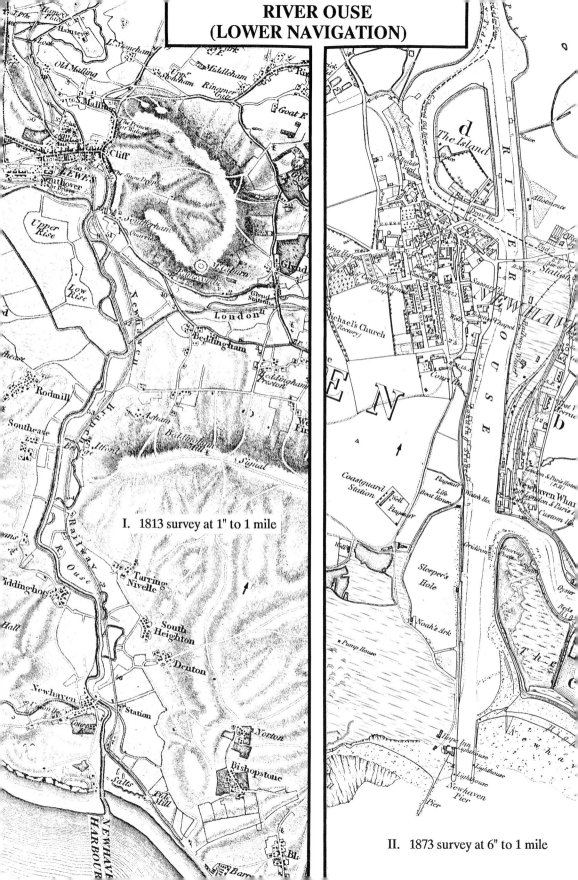

**RIVER OUSE
(LOWER NAVIGATION)**

I. 1813 survey at 1" to 1 mile

II. 1873 survey at 6" to 1 mile

The River Ouse was the most important Sussex river after the River Arun. Rising on the outskirts of St. Leonard's Forest, it flowed over 40 miles to its estuary at Newhaven. The river had been used by small boats since the seventeenth century and had been considered sufficiently important to form part of a grand scheme laid before the House of Lords in 1663 to link up the rivers between the Thames and Southampton to form one huge waterways network.

The Ouse (Lower Navigation) stretched from 40 chains north of Newhaven Bridge to Lewes Bridge (7 miles) and followed the winding course of the river, except for various cuts authorised under the 1791 Ouse Navigation Act. Previous to this Act, the river had only been navigable for small barges which were sailed or poled at favourable states of the tide. Horses were rarely employed at any time. The arrival of the London Brighton & South Coast Railway at Lewes in 1846, and its extension to Newhaven in 1847, enabled the navigation to act as a feeder to the railway in conveying chalk and clay from the pits to the cement factory at Asham or from the cement factory to the port. In 1898, the estimated traffic was slightly under 30,000 tons comprising imported Scandinavian timber, coal for the waterside gas works, chalk and cement. Regular commercial traffic decreased after World War I and ceased to Lewes in 1927, but cargo boats and sailing barges continued to use the river up to Southerham until the 1950s.

1. Newhaven Harbour is viewed north eastwards, with the South Downs in the background. The area in the foreground was known as Sleeper's Hole. This 1900 view shows three cross-channel steamers moored by the London & Paris Hotel with the chalk pit on Norton Hill at the right.

2. The London Brighton & South Coast Railway reached Newhaven in 1847 and in 1849 the cross-channel steamer service to Dieppe was transferred from Shoreham to the port. In 1852, the London & Paris Hotel was built on the quayside. (King Louis Philippe had to stay at the Bridge Hotel when he escaped from France after the Revolution in 1848). This view was drawn in 1871 when paddle steamers were heavily engaged in carrying victuals for Paris at the conclusion of the Franco-Prussian War.

3. Until 1784, the river could only be crossed at Newhaven by ferry. The timber drawbridge erected in that year had a 40ft opening. The fixed approach bridges were 35ft 5ins on the west side (where a toll house was erected on the quay) and 60ft to the bank on the east side. The two leaves of the centre section opened upwards. In 1864 the drawbridge was purchased for £4000 by the trustees of the Newhaven Harbour Board and the Lower Ouse Navigation and demolished in 1867.

4. The original bridge was replaced by a swing bridge lower down the river. The girders were made at the Phoenix Iron Works in Lewes. The bridge (shown here c.1900) which was in use from 1866 to 1974 had a swinging portion 150ft long and 27ft wide. It took eight men about three minutes to open the bridge and road traffic was halted for about 9 to 10 minutes whilst the gas main was disconnected and reconnected. The bridge was replaced by a modern swing bridge in November 1974 and the old bridge was demolished in 1976. It is ironical that it takes the same time to open and close the new bridge to allow shipping to pass as for the previous one.

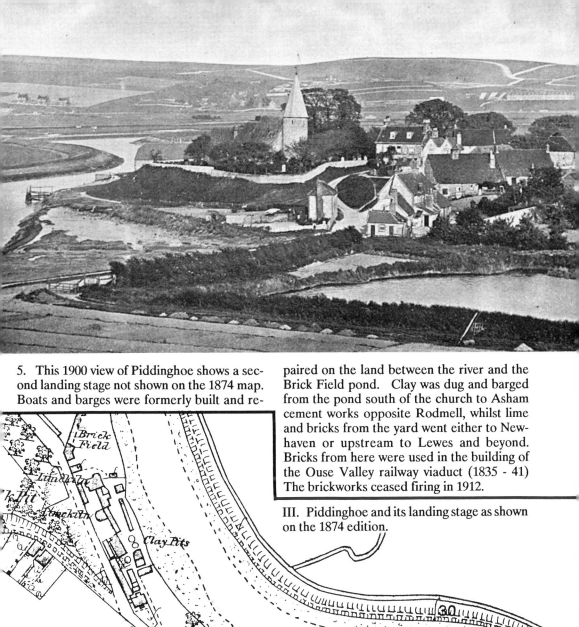

5. This 1900 view of Piddinghoe shows a second landing stage not shown on the 1874 map. Boats and barges were formerly built and repaired on the land between the river and the Brick Field pond. Clay was dug and barged from the pond south of the church to Asham cement works opposite Rodmell, whilst lime and bricks from the yard went either to Newhaven or upstream to Lewes and beyond. Bricks from here were used in the building of the Ouse Valley railway viaduct (1835 - 41) The brickworks ceased firing in 1912.

III. Piddinghoe and its landing stage as shown on the 1874 edition.

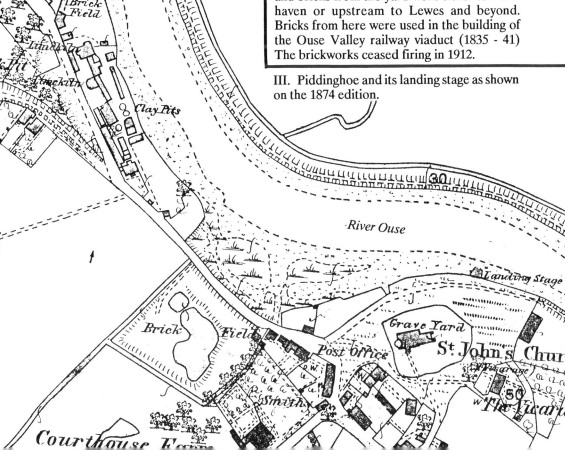

6. Small sailing barges were still in service between Lewes and the port of Newhaven in the 1930s. The barge shown was a double ended craft, with a single mast setting a sprit sail and carrying a high stack of well filled sacks.

7. Southerham Bridge was built in 1847 to carry the Lewes to Newhaven railway over the Ouse. It was a timber drawbridge to allow river traffic to pass and was similar to the bridge built over the River Arun at Ford in the previous year. The wooden bridge was replaced by the steel one depicted here. Its centre portion could be rolled back. This was a time absorbing and cumbersome business but by the 1930s the bridge was seldom opened. However, when the Southern Railway proposed to change from gas to electric lighting at Lewes Station, the gas company threatened to enforce their bridge rights by bringing their daily supplies of coal up by lighter instead of by train. The station remained lit by gas until after the 1948 railway nationalisation.

8. This is one of the last sailing barges to be moored above Southerham chalk pit in 1951. Although regular commercial traffic to Lewes had ceased by 1928, craft continued to come up to this mooring until 1955.

9. A painting by Alfred Bennet shows a sailing barge moored by Southerham Chalk Pit in 1887.

10. Southerham Chalk pits are viewed looking downstream in 1900. Commercial craft have since given way to pleasure craft.

11. This illustration of Lewes, drawn by Pollard in about 1820, was made from the timberyard, which was approached from South Street by Timberyard Lane.

12. This crane stood to the left of the dock seen in the previous picture and is seen in about 1834. Lewes Castle is in the centre. (Sussex Archaeological Society Coll.)

13. A snow (a type of brigantine) stands in the dock at Higham's Wharf, off South Street at Lewes, around 1855. The ship has not been positively identified but it may have been built at the Lewes Shipyard of Edward Chatfield. The dock has now been filled in but the houses were still identifiable in 1939.

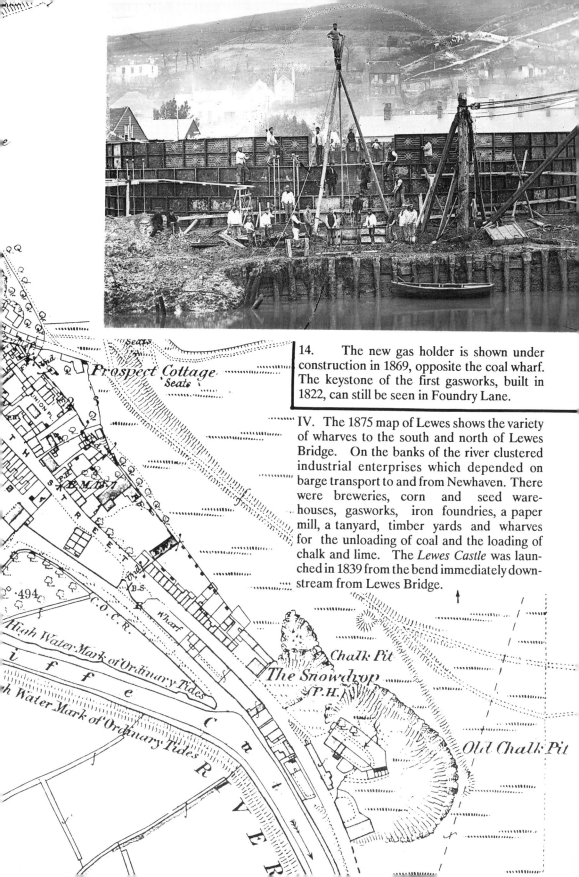

14. The new gas holder is shown under construction in 1869, opposite the coal wharf. The keystone of the first gasworks, built in 1822, can still be seen in Foundry Lane.

IV. The 1875 map of Lewes shows the variety of wharves to the south and north of Lewes Bridge. On the banks of the river clustered industrial enterprises which depended on barge transport to and from Newhaven. There were breweries, corn and seed warehouses, gasworks, iron foundries, a paper mill, a tanyard, timber yards and wharves for the unloading of coal and the loading of chalk and lime. The *Lewes Castle* was launched in 1839 from the bend immediately downstream from Lewes Bridge.

15.   Coal was brought up by barge from Newhaven for the Lewes Gas Light & Coke Company until 1927.   In the background can be seen the iron foundry of Ebenezer Morris, who was also chairman of the Poor Law Guardians.

16.   The launch of the 61 ton 60ft schooner *Lewes Castle* in 1839 from the yard of Messrs Rickman & Godlee.   This was the first sea going vessel built at Lewes.   The day was fine and the ceremony was watched by hundreds of spectators.   Besides sea-going ships many barges were also built for work on the river navigation.
(Sussex Archaeological Society Coll.)

17. A view from about 1868 shows the foundry and the Etna Iron Works to be connected by a drawbridge. On the right, beyond the steps of the Town Wharf, are corn and seed warehouses and on the left is The Bear Hotel, which was burnt down in 1918.

18. A similar view to the last picture is seen from Lewes bridge, thirty years later. The drawbridge, built by Burwood Godlee in 1839, has been replaced by a footbridge which now leads directly into Stevensons warehouse. Stevensons were corn and agricultural merchants and their name on the building can still be discerned in 1989. The Etna Ironworks was replaced in 1900 by the former Tabernacle Sunday School.

GLYNDE REACH

19. A barge, moored below Glynde Bridge, was photographed in about 1908. The last barge was towed up in 1928 when the method was to send two men down each bank to the junction with the Ouse and then haul the barges up by hand on the tide. Besides householders' needs, coal was required to fire the kilns at the nearby chalk pits.

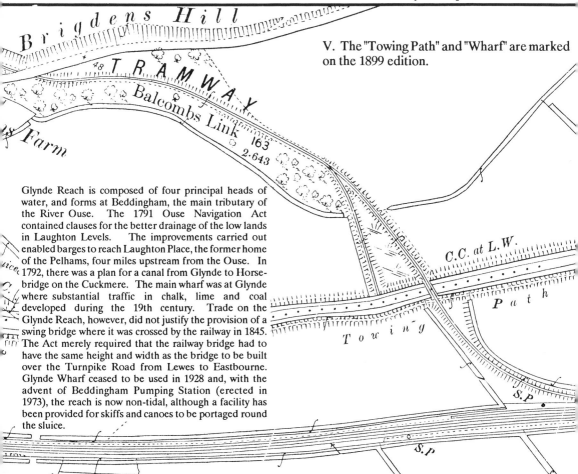

V. The "Towing Path" and "Wharf" are marked on the 1899 edition.

Glynde Reach is composed of four principal heads of water, and forms at Beddingham, the main tributary of the River Ouse. The 1791 Ouse Navigation Act contained clauses for the better drainage of the low lands in Laughton Levels. The improvements carried out enabled barges to reach Laughton Place, the former home of the Pelhams, four miles upstream from the Ouse. In 1792, there was a plan for a canal from Glynde to Horsebridge on the Cuckmere. The main wharf was at Glynde where substantial traffic in chalk, lime and coal developed during the 19th century. Trade on the Glynde Reach, however, did not justify the provision of a swing bridge where it was crossed by the railway in 1845. The Act merely required that the railway bridge had to have the same height and width as the bridge to be built over the Turnpike Road from Lewes to Eastbourne. Glynde Wharf ceased to be used in 1928 and, with the advent of Beddingham Pumping Station (erected in 1973), the reach is now non-tidal, although a facility has been provided for skiffs and canoes to be portaged round the sluice.

20. This 1940s view, taken at low tide, of the disused coal wharf at the right. The mooring posts shown on the left belonged to a wharf which was leased to the owners of the lime pit. In the background is Mount Caburn.

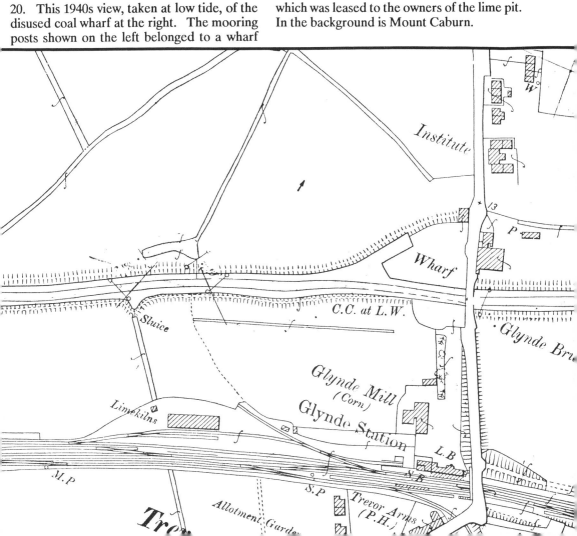

In 1884, the directors of the newly established Portland Cement Works at South Heighton, near Newhaven, decided to obtain a supply of gault clay from a pit east of the Decoy Wood and to the north of Glynde Reach. An automatic electrically operated supply system called telpherage had been recently invented and it was decided to build a telpher line - the first to be erected in England - to carry the clay over Glynde Reach to the railway station. The posts were on average 18ft above the ground. The experiment apparently soon failed because the 1899 Ordnance Survey shows that the line had been replaced by a tramway which crossed the reach on a wooden bridge. The clay pit and tramway ceased to be used around 1915 and the bridge was dismantled in 1935.

ON THE ARRIVAL OF THE TRAIN AT GLYNDE,

A Man bearing a Flag will be in attendance

TO CONDUCT THE COMPANY'S GUESTS

TO THE

ENGINE HOUSE.

Visitors are requested to post themselves ON THE

BANKS OF THE CANAL, whence they will have a

FULL VIEW OF THE

STARTING GEAR AND PLATFORM,

AND ALSO OF THE TRAINS.

THE LINE WILL BE FORMALLY OPENED

BY THE

Right Hon. Viscountess Hampden.

AFTER THE

OPENING CEREMONY,

A Man with a Flag will lead the Visitors to

THE LUNCHEON TENT,

FROM WHICH

A Good View of the Discharging End of the Line

AND THE

OPERATION OF TIPPING THE SKEPS

will be got; also a

Bird's-eye View of the Greater Part of the Line.

Those Visitors who prefer to walk on and examine the Line will find competent people to go with them.

A Flag will be hoisted at the Tent, and the Whistle of the Engine sounded FIFTEEN MINUTES BEFORE THE BEGINNING OF LUNCH The Flag will be lowered and the Whistle again sounded AT THE MOMENT OF THE CHAIR BEING TAKEN.

NOTE.—The Officers of the Company and others competent to explain the Working of the Line will wear Red Ribbons in their Button Holes.

21. At high tide the coal wharf and turning bay was, in this 1951 view, almost blocked by silt. The wharfinger's cottage is on the right.

OUSE (UPPER NAVIGATION)

The navigation stretched from Lewes Bridge to Upper Ryelands Bridge, between Balcombe and Haywards Heath. A map of 1724 indicates that small boats used a tributary stream to the powder mills and forge at Maresfield, above Shortbridge, where a flash lock had been built at the point where the stream joined the Ouse.

In 1788 William Jessop surveyed the river above Lewes and reported on how the river could be improved for navigation. Consequently, an Act of Parliament was passed in 1790 to make the Ouse navigable from Lewes to Hammer Bridge, near Cuckfield, with a branch to Shortbridge, near Fletching.

The contract for the work was let to Pinkertons, who were at that time also working with Jessop on the Basingstoke Canal. By April 1793, the river has been improved as far upstream as Sheffield Bridge, but the money being exhausted, the navigation was put in the hands of a receiver until further capital could be raised. In 1805, another one and a half miles and two locks were completed taking the navigation as far as Freshfield Bridge.

In 1806, the company obtained a further Act of Parliament which enabled it to raise a further £30,000 and repealed the section of the 1790 Act which required them to continue the navigation from Hammer Bridge to the far side of Cuckfield Parish. Work recommenced, the navigation reaching Lindfield in 1809 and finally Upper Ryelands Bridge in 1812.

The navigation from Lewes to Upper Ryelands Bridge was over 22 miles long and its 18 locks were built 53ft 8ins by 13ft 6ins to take barges up to 18 tons. The Ouse was an agricultural waterway, with an upstream traffic of bulk goods such as chalk, coal and stone for road repairs and a return traffic of agricultural produce.

Trade was at its busiest while the London to Brighton railway was under construction. The Wharf at Upper Ryelands Bridge was used from 1835 until 1841 for unloading materials for building the giant Balcombe Viaduct. After the railway was opened, there was some trade which passed upstream to be transferred to goods trains and vice versa but by 1846 this traffic was ended by the extensions of the railway from Brighton to Lewes.

By reducing its toll rates, the navigation was able to continue to profitably carry local traffic until the opening of the branch line from Lewes to Uckfield in 1858. A further reduction in the toll on coal failed to recover traffic lost to its competitor and in 1859 the company's boats ceased operation. The navigation above Lindfield ceased to be used after 1861 and the last barge reached the village in 1868. Occasionally barges and pleasure boats used the navigation above Lewes in the 1870s but by the time the railway was opened to East Grinstead in 1882, all water-borne traffic had ceased.

The New Oarsman's Guide described how in 1894 the locks were "now in a state of ruin, the channel of the upper reaches much obstructed by bushes and the navigation above Lewes wholly abandoned. An attempt has been made to introduce salmon, and the salmon ladders have been constructed through some of the old locks". It is interesting to note that mention was made of an old barge causing some obstruction "beyond Sharp's Lock and about half-way to Isfield". The authors suggested that the river could still be descended by canoes and small craft from Sheffield Park.

"There are 4 portages while tree branches and projecting shrubs in a narrow channel cause an occasional stoppage but there are no unsurmountable difficulties".

The enterprising countryside explorer can try to detect the locations of the former locks and wharves. Some have well preserved chambers and there are still signs of paddle gear and rotting timbers; some are little more than crumbling heaps of brick or stone while at places like Tester's and Gold Bridge, you will be well rewarded if you can discover sufficient evidence to visualise their former existence. The check list may prove helpful. If ever a waterway deserved the attention of volunteer labour to restore it, it is the Sussex Ouse. The former waterway traverses one of the most beautiful stretches of Sussex countryside and deserves to be restored. The Ouse Navigation Acts have never been repealed and as far as I can ascertain, the navigation above Lewes has never been officially abandoned.

Sheffield P'k Bridge	Stat. L. B. & S. C. R. Inn, Sheffield Arms (good) 1 mile. Launch at back of station down grass bank and through hedge.
Fletching Lock .	Portage, left bank. On a full river after rain the stream runs fast to Newick. Fletching ½ mile, left bank, has tomb of Gibbon.
Newick Bridge .	A short distance above, wooden debris of an old lock requires care if the stream is strong. Newick ¾ mile, right bank, Inn, Bull. Stat. L. B. & S. C. R. 1¾ mile right bank.
Sharp's Lock .	Gates gone and river runs through. Very narrow below, with awkward snags and bushes. About half-way to Isfield an old barge causes (1894) some obstruction.
Isfield Lock . .	Approach to lock and weir blocked by reeds (1894). Go on past weir, pull out at little sluice gate, hidden under bushes, left bank, and launch at foot of steep slope obliquely to the right.
Uckfield River Junc	Left bank. Once navigable to Uckfield (4 miles).
Isfield Bridge .	Stat. L. B. & S. C. R. ½ mile. Inn, Station Arms. Church has some brasses and monuments.
Railway Bridge .	House with boats to let just beyond, also very low road bridge, which, unless river is low, requires portage.
Barcombe Oil Mill Lock . . .	Converted into salmon-ladder. Portage right bank and over bridge.
Barcombe Mills L'k	Converted into salmon-ladder. Get permission to portage into private stream, right bank between house and mill. Stat. L. B. & S. C. R. Inn, Station Arms, right bank below mill. Tide flows up to this.
Railway Bridge Hamsey Lock .	No gates, tide flows through. Long backwater on left, below.
Currie's Bridge ? Railway Bridge	"The Deanery" on left.
Lewes Bridge -	Stat. L. B. & S. C. R. Hotel, White Hart. Land at bridge or at Boat Club left bank ¼ mile below. Ruined castle in which is interesting museum. High chalk downs below on left bank.
Railway Bridge -	Round next bend is fine view of Lewes and its picturesque castle.
Swing Bridge Piddinghoe Church Entrance to B'kwat'r Newhaven Bridge -	Right bank. Keep straight on. Land at bridge, right bank. Strong tide. Inn, Bridge, near. Landlord has large shed for housing boats. Stats. L. B. & S. C. R. Hotel, London and Paris, left bank ⅜ mile below bridge, also Sheffield Arms near Pier, right bank. Small town. Fine breakwater, fort and cliffs are objects of interest.
Mouth of River	

23. Since 1781 the bridge has been reconstructed as this 1951 view illustrates. In 1808 the overhanging pedestrian pavement was added to the north side but it was not until 1932 that a similar pavement was made on the south side of the bridge and the stone parapets were replaced with iron railings.

24. Here we see much of the riverside industry above Lewes Bridge in about 1870. The railway line to Uckfield opened in 1868 and closed in 1969 (and now dismantled), crosses the Ouse and cuts across the timber yards and sawmill. Offham Chalk Pits are in the background.

22. Cliffe Bridge, Lewes, was built in 1727. This watercolour by James Lambert was painted in 1782 looking upstream.

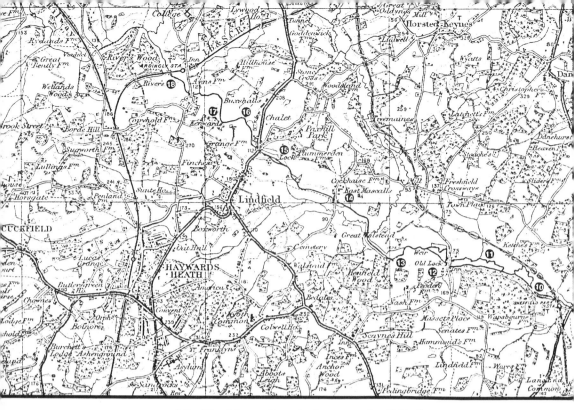

VI. The Upper Ouse is shown on the 1920 1" scale map, the imposed numbers referring to the table below. The lower right corner of the map above is continuous with the upper left part of the section opposite.

	LOCK	GRID REF.	DATE BUILT	DATE CLOSED	STATE (1989)	ACCESS (1989)
1	Hamsey	407119	1791	1870	B	D
2	Barcombe Mills (Lower)	433148	1791	1870	A	D
3	Barcombe Mills (Upper)	434147	1791	1870	A	D
4	Barcombe Oil Mills	440168	1792	1870	A	E
5	Isfield	441187	1792	1868	B	F
6	Sharps Bridge	443206	1792	1868	B	E
7	Gold Bridge	427216	1793	1868	C	D
8	Fletching	424231	1793	1868	A	D
9	Iron Gate	409228	1793	1868	B	F
10	Bacon Wish	398241	1798	1868	A	E
11	Polebay	393242	1799	1868	A	D
12	Freshfield	385245	1799	1868	A	D
13	Henfield Wood	374245	1809	1868	C	F
14	East Mascall's	366254	1809	1868	C	D
15	Pim's	355262	1809	1868	A	D
16	Fulling Mill	350268	1812	1861	B	F
17	Tester's	346268	1812	1861	C	D
18	Riverswood	336275	1812	1861	A	F

A - Chamber Intact
B - Traces
C - No Trace
D - Easy
E - Fair
F - Difficult

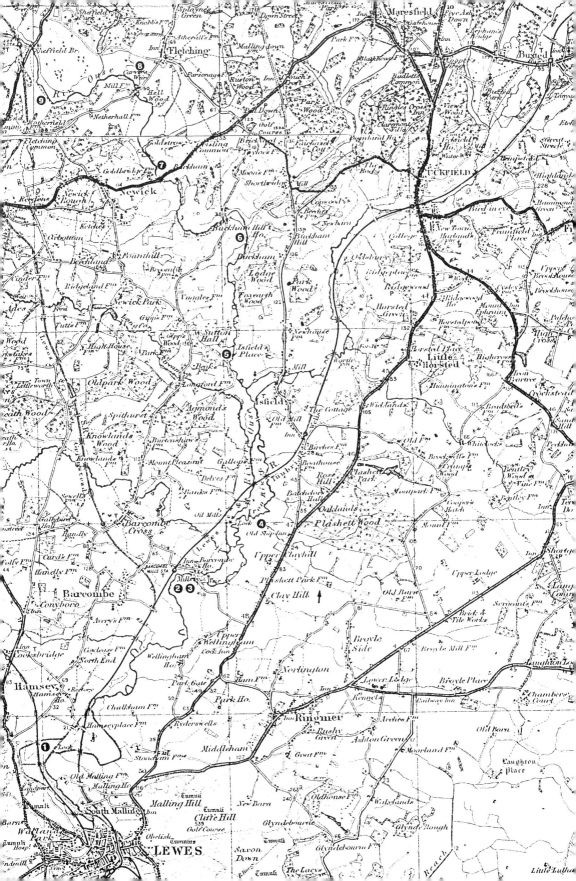

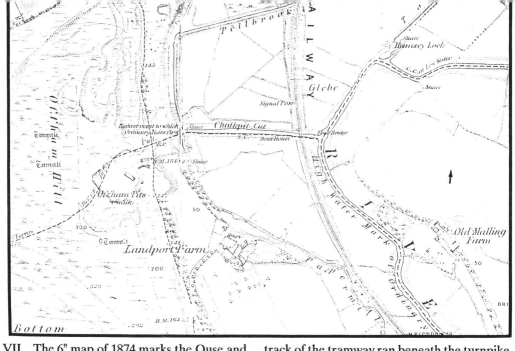

VII.   The 6" map of 1874 marks the Ouse and associated cuts.   The Offham Chalkpit Cut was made in about 1790 and the tramway to carry chalk from the pit, 150ft above river level, to the new cut was opened in March 1809.   The track of the tramway ran beneath the turnpike road (now the A275), through twin tunnels which are still visible, just over one mile north of Lewes.

VIII.   The 25" scale 1874 survey details the inclined tramway, the wharf being at the lower (right hand) end.

25.   Barcombe Mill House is portrayed in 1909.   The building was built in 1870 of pitch pine with a semi-classic facade and was burnt down in March 1939. It was a corn mill until WWI and was used in the 1920s as a button factory. At the left is the private road between the toll bridge and Pike's Bridge.   Barges moored at the wharf marked by the mooring posts.   Today only a plaque above the toll bridge and a grass covered area indicates the site of the mill house and the railway siding.

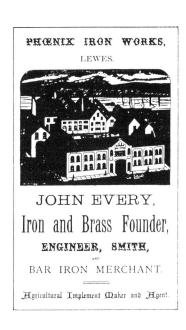

PHŒNIX IRON WORKS,
LEWES.

JOHN EVERY,
Iron and Brass Founder,
ENGINEER, SMITH,
AND
BAR IRON MERCHANT.

Agricultural Implement Maker and Agent.

26.   Pike's Bridge crosses the lock-cut between the lower and upper locks. G. D. Johnston, the Sussex archaeologist reported in 1909 that the lock gates at Barcombe Mills, which were chained together, were "nearly falling to pieces". Fish ladders have been incorporated into the lock chambers to allow sea trout to leap upstream.

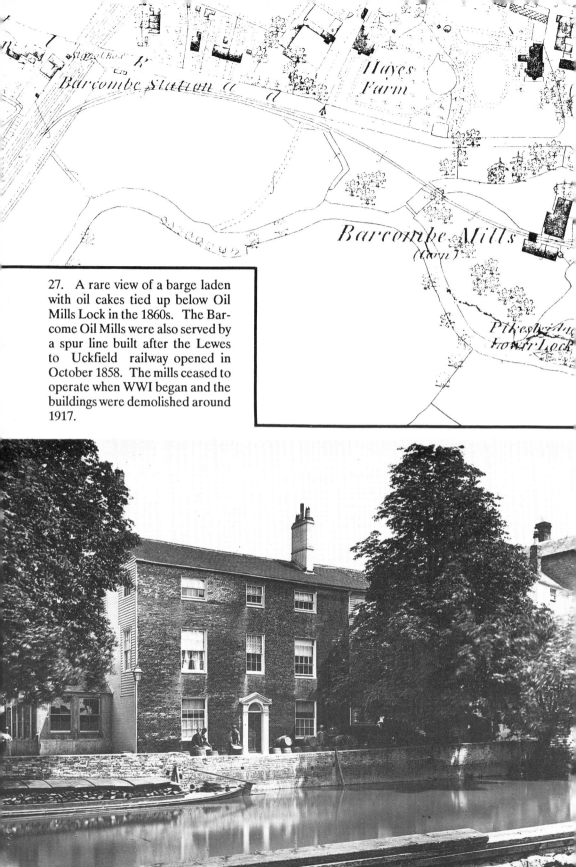

27. A rare view of a barge laden with oil cakes tied up below Oil Mills Lock in the 1860s. The Barcome Oil Mills were also served by a spur line built after the Lewes to Uckfield railway opened in October 1858. The mills ceased to operate when WWI began and the buildings were demolished around 1917.

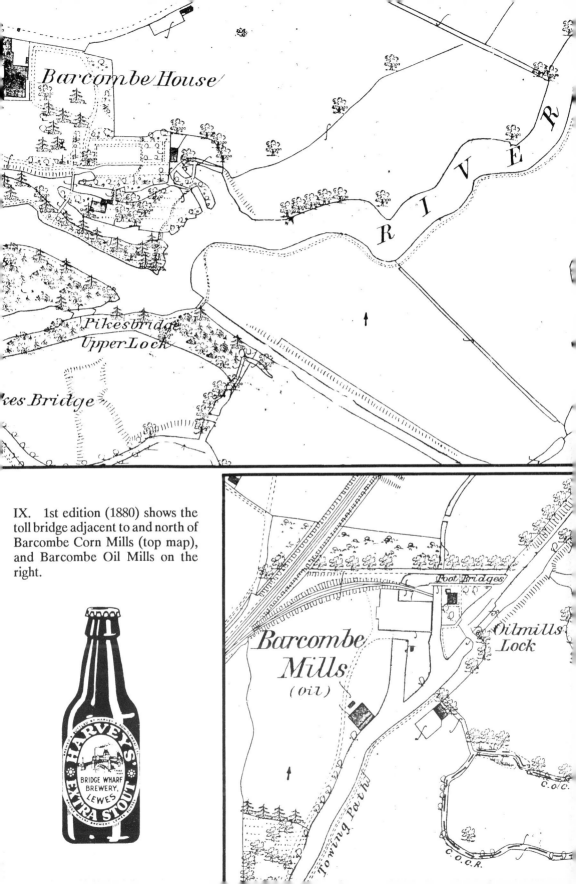

Barcombe House

RIVER

Pikesbridge
Upper Lock

...kes Bridge

IX. 1st edition (1880) shows the toll bridge adjacent to and north of Barcombe Corn Mills (top map), and Barcombe Oil Mills on the right.

Foot Bridges

Oilmills Lock

Barcombe Mills
(oil)

Towing Path

C.O.C.

C.O.O.R.

HARVEY'S
EXTRA STOUT
BRIDGE WHARF
BREWERY,
LEWES

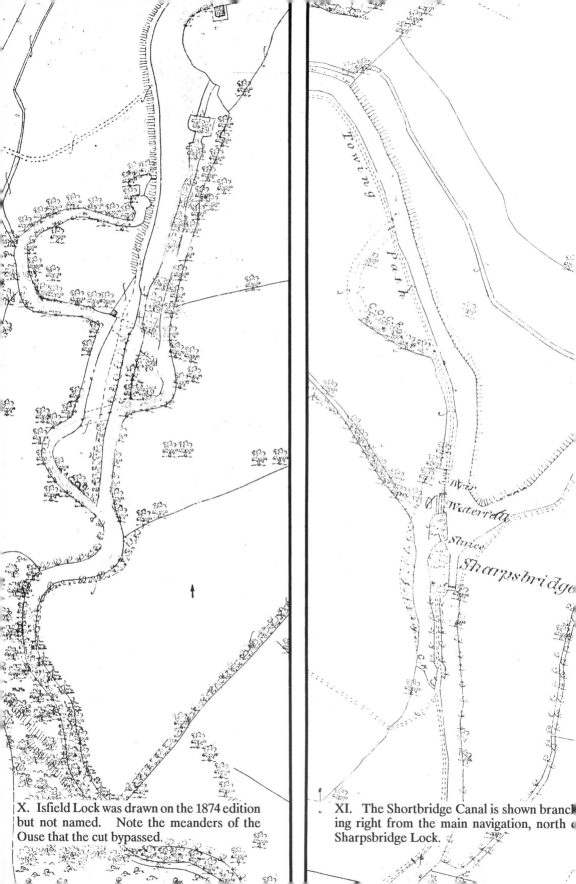

X. Isfield Lock was drawn on the 1874 edition but not named. Note the meanders of the Ouse that the cut bypassed.

XI. The Shortbridge Canal is shown branching right from the main navigation, north of Sharpsbridge Lock.

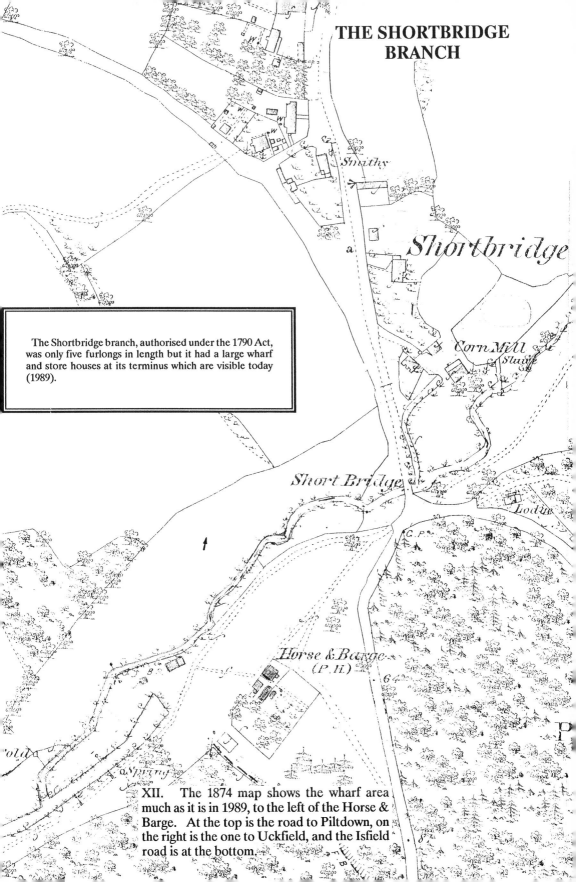

THE SHORTBRIDGE BRANCH

Smithy

Shortbridge

a

Corn Mill
Sluice

The Shortbridge branch, authorised under the 1790 Act, was only five furlongs in length but it had a large wharf and store houses at its terminus which are visible today (1989).

Short Bridge

Lodge

C.P.

Horse & Barge
(P.H.)

64

Spring

XII.   The 1874 map shows the wharf area much as it is in 1989, to the left of the Horse & Barge.   At the top is the road to Piltdown, on the right is the one to Uckfield, and the Isfield road is at the bottom.

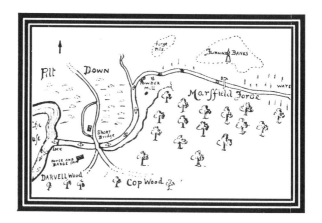

XIII. Maresfield Powder Mills were established in the 16th century on a tributary stream some two and a half miles from the main river. A map dated 1724 indicates a flash lock at the entrance to the tributary which suggests that gunpowder was carried downstream to Lewes. Although the toll rates authorised by Parliament between 1790 and 1814 do not specifically list "gunpowder", this is not conclusive since gunpowder appears to have been categorized as "other goods" on several navigations. A serious explosion in 1854 caused the mills to be abandoned and the wooden buildings dismantled. Shortbridge corn mill was not built until 1872, by when the wharf had been closed.

28. The Horse & Barge Public House which stood above the wharf may have existed before the navigation was open. This photograph was taken in 1930 when it had reverted to a private residence. The house was sold again by auction in 1983.

29. Coal and groceries were unloaded at the wharf for Uckfield (2 miles) and loaded mainly with agricultural produce to be taken down to Lewes (10 miles).

30. The building to the right of the wharf was formerly used as a storehouse and as a stable for the barge horse.

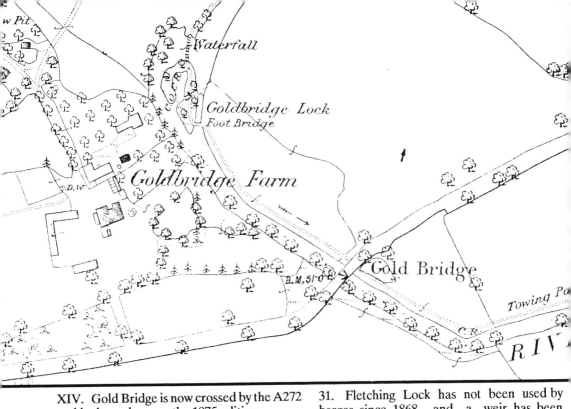

XIV. Gold Bridge is now crossed by the A272 and is shown here on the 1875 edition.

31. Fletching Lock has not been used by barges since 1868, and a weir has been substituted by the water authority for the lock gates, which allows the river to flow through the old lock chamber as seen in 1989.

32. The Sloop Inn, by Freshfield Lock, was where navigators and bargees drank their ale over a period of seventy years. Before WW2 a narrow hump backed bridge here carried the road over the canal cut. Freshfield Lock is on the opposite side of the road.

33. The main stream of the river runs through the crumbling brick walls of Polebay Lock in 1989.

34. Bacon Wish Lock is the only lock to have retained its original bridge. The chamber floor has been concreted and a sluice built in place of the upper gate.

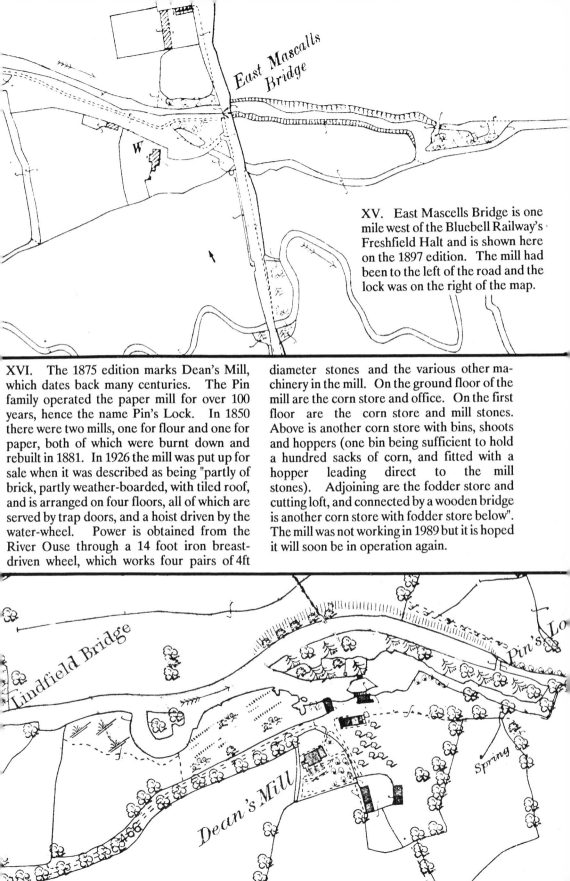

XV. East Mascells Bridge is one mile west of the Bluebell Railway's Freshfield Halt and is shown here on the 1897 edition. The mill had been to the left of the road and the lock was on the right of the map.

XVI. The 1875 edition marks Dean's Mill, which dates back many centuries. The Pin family operated the paper mill for over 100 years, hence the name Pin's Lock. In 1850 there were two mills, one for flour and one for paper, both of which were burnt down and rebuilt in 1881. In 1926 the mill was put up for sale when it was described as being "partly of brick, partly weather-boarded, with tiled roof, and is arranged on four floors, all of which are served by trap doors, and a hoist driven by the water-wheel. Power is obtained from the River Ouse through a 14 foot iron breast-driven wheel, which works four pairs of 4ft diameter stones and the various other machinery in the mill. On the ground floor of the mill are the corn store and office. On the first floor are the corn store and mill stones. Above is another corn store with bins, shoots and hoppers (one bin being sufficient to hold a hundred sacks of corn, and fitted with a hopper leading direct to the mill stones). Adjoining are the fodder store and cutting loft, and connected by a wooden bridge is another corn store with fodder store below". The mill was not working in 1989 but it is hoped it will soon be in operation again.

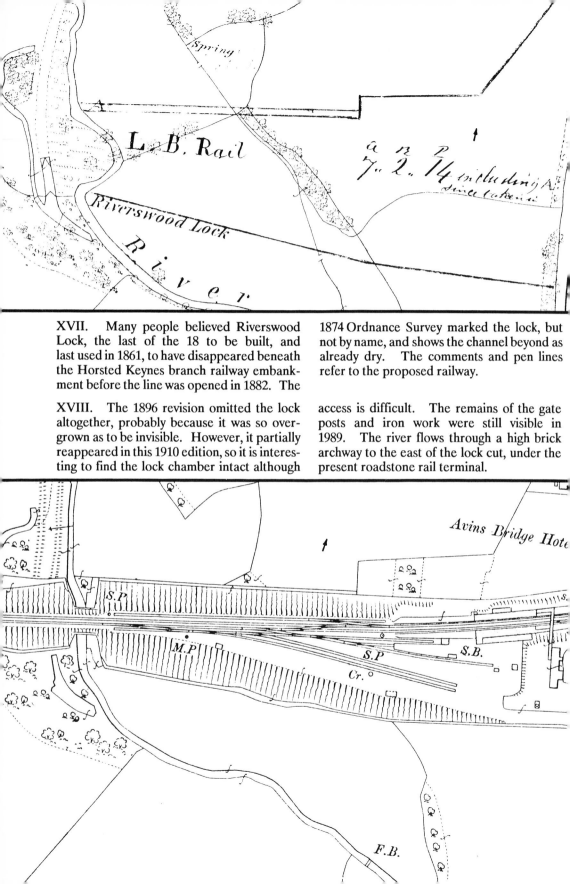

XVII.   Many people believed Riverswood Lock, the last of the 18 to be built, and last used in 1861, to have disappeared beneath the Horsted Keynes branch railway embankment before the line was opened in 1882. The 1874 Ordnance Survey marked the lock, but not by name, and shows the channel beyond as already dry.   The comments and pen lines refer to the proposed railway.

XVIII.   The 1896 revision omitted the lock altogether, probably because it was so overgrown as to be invisible. However, it partially reappeared in this 1910 edition, so it is interesting to find the lock chamber intact although access is difficult.   The remains of the gate posts and iron work were still visible in 1989.   The river flows through a high brick archway to the east of the lock cut, under the present roadstone rail terminal.

35. Balcombe Wharf was opened in 1812 and was the terminus of the navigation. This was where construction materials, brought up the Ouse Navigation, were unloaded into carts and then carried to the foot of the viaduct during the building of the London to Brighton Railway. Until the opening of the Lewes branch line in 1846, railway goods were also unloaded and taken down to Lindfield and Lewes.

36. The wharfinger's cottage, built in about 1812, at the terminus of the navigation at Upper Ryelands Bridge is shown in 1989. Adjacent are the slate roofed red brick cottages built for the workers constructing the viaduct. The Balcombe Viaduct carries the London to Brighton Railway over the Ouse Valley. Completed in 1841 it has 37 arches, is 96 feet high and 1475 feet long. The engineer was John Raistrick. Four stone pavilions at each end form an attractive feature.

RIVER CUCKMERE

The River Cuckmere rises near Heathfield and enters the English Channel at Cuckmere Haven. It is difficult to establish just when and what amount of barge traffic used the river. The written records are few but unusual. The inscription on a gravestone in the churchyard at Alfriston indicates that John Lower was the first person to navigate the river to Alfriston. Since he died in August 1801 aged 66, it seems probably that barge traffic began about, or soon after, 1770 when it would have been feasible for small coasting vessels carrying coal from Newhaven to have been unloaded at the haven.

In 1801 **The Adventure** owned by William Stevens of Berwick and **The Good Will** owned by Sarah Lower of Alfriston were registered as trading between the Haven and Alfriston. Traffic could ascend the river on the tide as far as Berwick where there was a wharf at Sherman's Bridge, and the 1819 Act for a new bridge directed that it should allow the passage of barges 10ft wide.

The main cargoes carried by barge were sea shingle (for repairing the roads), sand, seaweed, chalk and coal which was brought from Newhaven. Traffic was light as Alfriston village boasted only ten houses in 1833 "of the humblest description". In 1846 the Commissioners of the Cuckmere Levels straightened the river between Exceat Bridge and the sea, which would have allowed normal high tides to flow to Sessingham Bridge, Arlington. Mr Major Vidler, however, reported in 1847, that after surveying the river to Horsebridge, he had found the entire bed was, in many places, filled with "decayed weeds and underwood". Vidler recommended the installation of three sets of gates between Sessingham and Michelham Mill, and it was the implementation of this proposal that accounts for three locks being marked on the 6" Ordnance Survey of 1870, between Longbridge and Michelham Priory. These were in reality sluice gates or penfolds, and were never used to assist boats in ascending the river above Berwick.

In 1909 Arthur Beckett wrote that only small boats float upon the Cuckmere "though now and then, when the tide is up a huge barge, ugly and cumbersome, is brought up from the river mouth". Commercial traffic ceased in 1915.

XIX. The entrance to Cuckmere Haven as it appeared on the 1" scale Ordnance Survey in 1813. The railway opened, in 1846, was superimposed on later editions, but not the straightening of the river up to Exceat, which was also carried out in 1846. The barracks on each side of the river were intended to house troops defending the coastline against a Napoleonic invasion, but their main task was to try to apprehend smugglers. Until the river was straightened between Exceat Bridge and Cuckmere Haven, its sinuosities made navigation by barge very difficult. Even above Exceat Bridge, sharp bends often caused a barge to go aground.

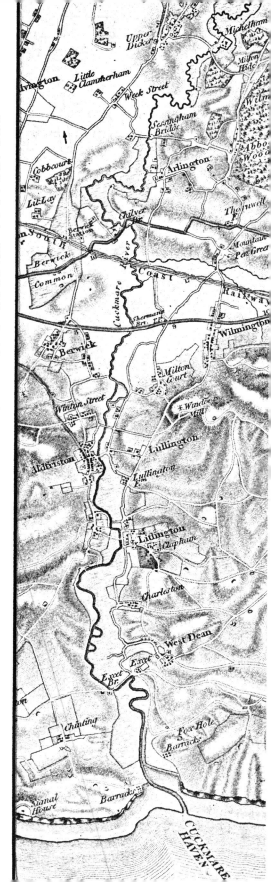

37. High tide at Cuckmere Haven is viewed from the east in 1931.   In the late 18th and much of the 19th centuries, harbour ploughs were used to remove the shingle blocking the river mouth. John Ellis was paid £10 p.a. from 1803 to 1809 (and probably for other years as well) to keep it open.   In the late 1930s, a groyne was built on the west side of the mouth, which caused the outfall to come out straight ahead and the inner pool (shown as full of water), to be banked off from the river.   Except for the odd occasions when a gale caused the sea to break through the shingle bank, the river's outflow used to filter through the beach.

38. A lightly loaded barge is moored below the footbridge at Alfriston in approximately 1910. The last barge to be berthed at the wharf was the *Iona* which made her final voyage down to the sea in 1915.   Until the late 1930s there was what was described in the Sussex County Magazine as "a comfortably old fashioned wooden footbridge across the Cuckmere at Alfriston".   However, the advent of the Cuckmere Catchment Board caused the river banks to be raised, the wharf to vanish and the bridge to be replaced with one four feet higher and four inches narrower.

39. Pleasure boats could be hired from the site of the wharf in the 1920s and E. V. Lucas writing in 1935 stated that "only the other day" at Hellingly, you could paddle for a mile in a punt or canadian canoe from the old water mill.

XX. The wharf shown on the 1874 map was upstream of the white railed footbridge. It was probably built early in the 19th century when consideration was also being given to extending the navigation from Longbridge to Horsebridge.

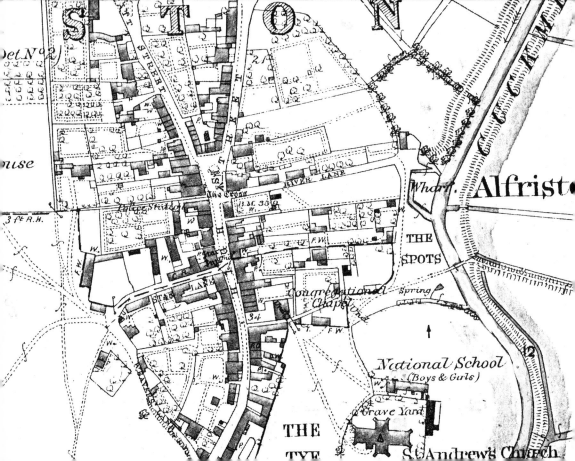

PEVENSEY LEVELS

The constant eastward drift of shingle has always threatened to block or alter the outlet of Sussex rivers. New harbour entrances had to be made for every Sussex port in the 18th century. Where there was insuficient trade, the harbour was simply abandoned. Such was the case at Pevensey, a cinque port, which ceased to operate from about the time of the Norman Conquest. By 1750 the outlet to the sea from the Pevensey Levels had become impracticable for small boats, and nowadays it is discharged through culverts beneath the beach. In the 17th Century, however, the great expense of land transport made any available form of land transport for the iron industry highly desirable, and Ernest Straker in his book "Wealden Iron" mentions how iron was brought down the maze of marsh channels in winter time. Barges were loaded at places like Chilthurst Bridge on the Nunningham Stream. A deed of 1667 included the right to carry iron in boats from Kitchenham Forge to Boreham Bridge as well as the power to cleanse and scour. The industry declined towards the close of the 18th century. Exports of cannon from Hastings ceased in 1789 by which time all but three of the Sussex iron furnaces had closed. Barge traffic on the Levels would have ceased about this time. The reports of the Commissioners of Pevensey Levels make no reference to water-borne carriage, but in 1842 they agreed that a maintenance barge should be built for use on the dykes.

40. This view of Pevensey Levels and the castle around 1910 indicates that punts were employed for cutting osiers.

XXI. This 1813 map of Pevensey Harbour is scaled at 1" to 1 mile. Note the line of Martello Towers which had been completed by 1810. Pevensey Levels were, and still are, a criss cross of streams, along which there was only limited navigation.

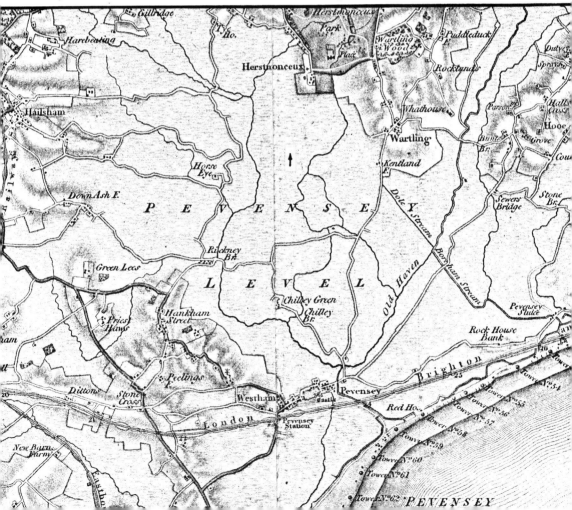

ROTHER NAVIGATION

The Eastern Rother rises near Rotherfield and was navigable from very early times from Rye, past Appledore and round the north of the Isle of Oxney to Newenden, Bodiam, Udiam and beyond. The Romans certainly used it to Bodiam and later it was navigable, for small boats, at least to Etchingham. Records exist of the carriage by water of stone for the building of Bodiam Castle in the 14th century, and of the shipment of mid - 16th century cargoes of iron from Udiam and from Bodiam.

There was also trade to Rolvenden from Maytham Wharf and to Tenterden from Smallhythe. In about 1695, the course of the Rother was shortened by some five miles by bringing it round to the south of the Isle of Oxney, the old north channel becoming the Reading Sewer. The Scots Float sluice and lock were completed in 1736 and rebuilt in 1844.

The navigation of the river and its tributaries was mainly by Rye sailing barges about 45ft x 12ft, drawing 2ft 9ins, and carrying some 20 tons. In about 1800 there seems to have been navigation to Appledore and Reading Street; to Maytham wharf, Newenden and Bodiam; to Small-hythe; and up the Newmill Channel towards Tenterden.

A pamphlet of 1802 says: "..... previous to the last ten years, three barges only were employed on the Rother navigations. Owing to the increased and still increasing demand for manures, fuel, and mendment for the roads, there are actually at this time no less than sixteen barges employed, chiefly in conveying those commodities".

The Parliamentary Acts of 1826 and 1830 laid certain obligations upon the Commissioners of the Rother Levels to maintain navigation between Scots Float and Bodiam Bridge, and a minimum bridge headroom of 5ft, although they were not empowered to collect tolls. Towing was by men; there was no horse path. Iron shod poles or quants were much used to push or punt the barges round the bends as they came up on the tide and to help them turn in these restricted waters.

Navigation continued up the Rother to Newenden and Maytham until the early 1930s. In 1933, land drainage needs were given priority over navigation above Scots Float. In 1981 the Southern Water Authority decided to replace Scots Float Sluice with a more modern installation which was built downstream in 1986. The former sluice was demolished in 1987.

XXII. A new harbour was begun at Rye in the 1720s but not opened until 1787. This new outlet for the Rother was made by turning the Rother and Brede from its previous course, building a navigable sluice to control the tides and forming a new channel and harbour at Pett Level. It had been open for less than six months when it had to be abandoned due to its mouth becoming blocked by shingle; consequently the former channel of the Rother had to be reopened. The scale is 1" to 1 mile.

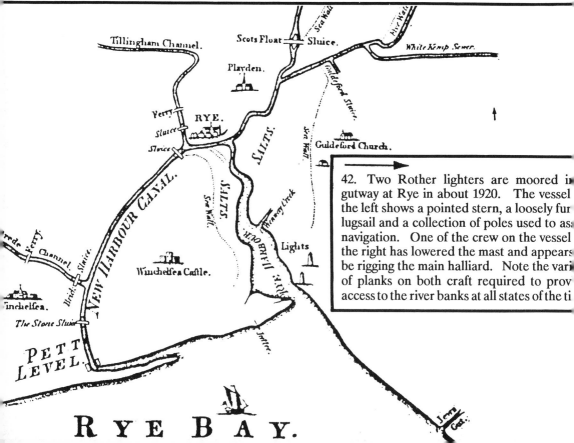

42. Two Rother lighters are moored in gutway at Rye in about 1920. The vessel the left shows a pointed stern, a loosely fur lugsail and a collection of poles used to ass navigation. One of the crew on the vessel the right has lowered the mast and appears be rigging the main halliard. Note the vari of planks on both craft required to prov access to the river banks at all states of the ti

41. The lighthouse at the entrance to Rye Harbour and the River Rother photographed in about 1912.

43. Rye Swing Bridge carried the Rye & Hastings branch of the South Eastern Railway. The bridge was swung by means of spur and bevel wheels and took two men under three minutes to complete the operation. The Rye Harbour commissioners received £10,000 compensation for the obstruction to the navigation. This view shows the bridge when it was opened by the Lord Mayor of London in 1851. The two windmills stood on Playden Heights, the smock mill being demolished around 1884. The bridge was demolished in 1903 and replaced by a double track fixed span bridge which provided sufficient headroom to allow the passage of unrigged barges or those with falling masts.

45. Barges on the Rother had to be under 45ft long and 12ft beam to pass through the tidal lock at Scots Float. It was erected in 1844 by William Cubitt and seen here looking downstream in 1955.

46. The bridge across the river by Iden Lock was built in 1808 to carry the military road from Rye to Hythe. This 1925 view shows a barge and pleasure boat below the bridge which has subsequently been rebuilt.

---

44. Scots Float Sluice (also known as Star Lock after the adjacent inn) was completed in 1736 as part of the new Rye Harbour project, which was not finished until 1787. The sluice was necessary for both drainage and navigational purposes, but it reduced the flow of the tide to the upper reaches, and in 1806 John Rennie described Scots Float sluice as being "very inconvenient and ill adapted to the present vessels which navigate the Rother". After the gates were damaged by an exceptionally high spring tide in 1812, the tidal flow reached Bodiam for the first time for many years. When the sluice was rebuilt in 1813, its low cross beams prevented barges from entering except at low tide. A law suit in 1819 was required to obtain a ruling that the sluice was a nuisance to navigation, but even after the Rye Harbour Acts of 1830 and 1833 had been passed it was not until 1844 that the sluice and lock were adequately rebuilt. This aerial view of Scots Float Sluice was taken in about 1960.

47. The sails of the Rye barges were in various shades of brown and brick-red. Owing to the many bends in the river the barges viewed downstream were never in line and occasionally they would seem to meet and pass one another, whereas in fact they were on different stretches of water.

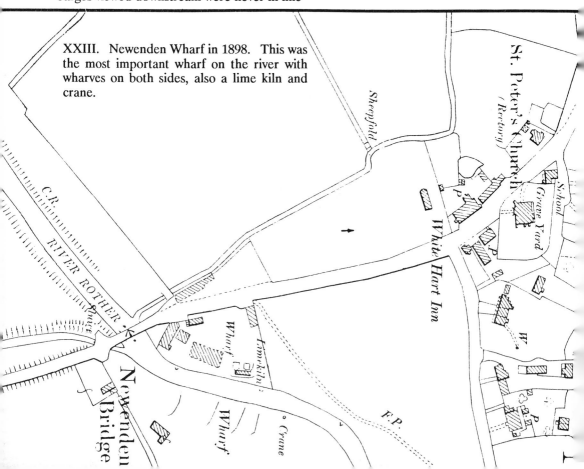

XXIII. Newenden Wharf in 1898. This was the most important wharf on the river with wharves on both sides, also a lime kiln and crane.

48. Newenden Wharf is seen soon after the turn of the century. The principal cargoes were agricultural produce, coal and timber; also shingle from the beach for road repairs. Much of the timber was for the sawmill on the left of this picture where a steam engine can be seen which was used to drive the saws.

49. Here we witness a Rye barge, moored on the north bank at Newenden, being unloaded on a bright wintry day in about 1900. The length and precarious nature of the gang-plank required the bargees to have not only strength but a steady nerve. Wooden shafts have been pushed into the bed of the river and lashed against the boat to keep it stationary.

50. A closer view of the man who had to push the wheelbarrow. From picture 49 it appears that empty barrows were pulled. The centre of the bridge, built in 1706, marks the county boundary between Sussex and Kent.

51. Bodiam Bridge and Castle as drawn in 1817. The derelict sailing barge lies at the mooring above the bridge. Although this was the normal limit of navigation, it is evident from the height of the bridge's central arch, built in 1796, that provision was made for barge traffic which in favourite conditions could proceed upstream.

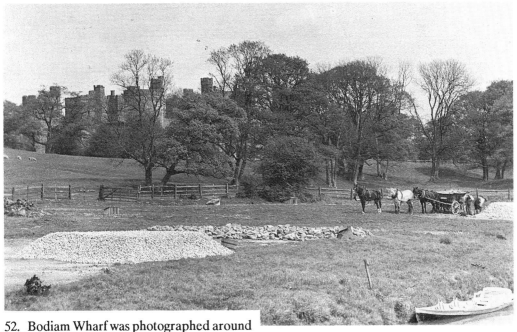

52. Bodiam Wharf was photographed around 1900. The castle was built in the 14th century in the reign of Richard II and dismantled during the Civil Wars only to be partially restored by Lord Curzon in the early 1920s.

53.　　Bodiam Wharf was north-east of the bridge and is seen in about 1910. Note the selection of iron-shod poles leaning against the mast, which had to be used to manoeuvre such vessels in restricted waters.

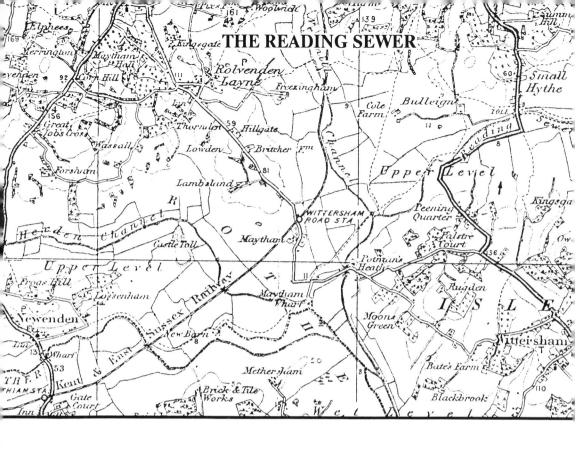

54. Here, in the 1890s, we witness the unloading of a lug sail barge from Rye at Smallhythe Wharf. Smallhythe Place, the home of actress Dame Ellen Terry (1847 - 1928), stands in the background. Smallhythe (pop. 1931 223) was the port for Tenterden (pop. 1931 3,431). It had no railway station until 1903 and relied on the Rother to bring its supply of coal, hop poles and groceries.

55. The wharf at Smallhythe in 1989.

56. The toll bridge leading from the Isle of Oxney to Smallhythe around 1900. Motor vehicles had to pay sixpence to pass in the 1930s.

XXIV. The 1920 survey enlarged to 1.5" to 1 mile, shows Maytham Wharf located on the Hexden Channel. It served the village of Rolvenden, over two miles distant. The lime kilns were closed towards the end of the 19th century, and the waterway lost some traffic when the Rother Valley Railway was opened from Robertsbridge to Rolvenden in 1900. Barges ascended the Rother to Blackwall Bridge, and took the north west branch up to Potman's Heath and the Reading Sewer to Smallhythe. The Reading Sewer formed the northern boundary of the Isle of Oxney and was part of the navigable channel from Appledore to Newenden. The wharves at Potman's Heath, Maytham and Smallhythe ceased to be used in the early 1930s.

The Reading Sewer is formed by the ancient channel of the river Rother which formerly flowed from below Maytham Wharf, round the northern side of the Isle of Oxney and past Smallhythe to Appledore. However, the inexorable effects of the shingle drift which had changed the fortunes of Winchelsea and Rye were also felt up the tidal reaches of the Rother, so that by 1736 the old channel was blocked by silt, causing serious flooding. It became necessary to form a new cut for the water through Wittersam Level whereby, according to Kent historian Hasted, "the course of the river for the space of five miles or more became inverted, and instead of running from Maytham to Smallhythe and Reading eastward, now (1797) runs from thence into the new channel along the southern side of the island".

XXV. Potman's Heath Wharf was south-east of Wittersham Road station and seen on the 1908 edition.

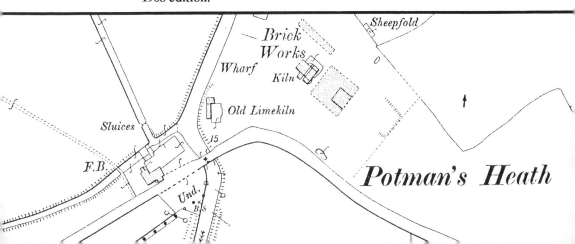

57. A barge sails on the Brede between Rye and Winchelsea near the turn of the century. This part of the waterway, together with the River Rother from Rye to Iden and the two sections of the military canal, formed the second line of defence against Napoleon's plan to invade Romney Marsh.

The Brede was navigable from very early times. In the 15th century lead purchased in London was being shipped up the tidal river from Rye to Sedlescombe for the Lady Chapel of Battle Abbey. During the Tudor period until 1766 there was an iron furnace in the village of Brede and it is known that from 1747 to 1766 barges came up the river from Strand Wharf, Rye, loaded with iron ore for the furnaces and with groceries for the village, returning laden with guns which were manufactured at the iron works. This could be dangerous work. Miles Chandler had both his legs broken and was later killed while loading guns at the wharf. In 1770, the iron furnace was converted into gunpowder mills. Severe explosions took place in 1778, 1787 and 1808 and the powder traffic had ceased by 1825.

The river formed part of the outlet to the new harbour at Rye which had to be abandoned in 1787, after being open for less than six months, due to its mouth being blocked by shingle. Consequently, in 1788, a navigable sluice was built by Bridge to improve the draught at low water. By 1808, the lock had fallen into ruin. It was repaired by the Royal Staff Corps who had been employed in building the defensive works along the Brede between Rye and Winchelsea. The western section from Winchelsea to Cliff End was linked to the Brede, but it was not used for public navigation, and in 1814 the flood gates and swivel bridge were replaced by a dam over which

58. Soldiers approach Winchelsea along the Royal Military Road in 1817. The Strand Gate is visible high on the hillside in the centre, to the left of the carriage. The military road was opened as a toll road in 1812 and is on the north side of the Brede Navigation which can be seen on the left. The water on the right is the back drain. The parapet forming the defence work between the road and the navigation appears not to have been built to any great extent at this point.

the road to Reed's Batteries and Winchelsea Beach was carried.

The Rye Harbour Act of 1833 required the Commissioners of Sewers for the Levels of Brede and Pett to maintain Brede sluice and the river navigable for barges to Brede Bridge (8 miles from Rye).

The navigation was effectively closed in 1933 when land drainage needs were given priority over the maintenance of a navigable depth, although local historian L. A. Vidler stated (in October 1935) that river barges still used the wharves at Winchelsea, Snailham and Brede Bridge.

59. This building, by Brede Bridge, and on the south bank of the river, formerly served as a warehouse and alehouse for the adjoining wharf. It was the more or less invariable winter floods, like those which occurred in 1909, which halted barge traffic due to the lack of headroom beneath the bridges at Winchelsea.

60. The Rye barge *Victoria* is seen at the wharf above Brede Bridge in 1923. Coal was unloaded by the steam crane into wagons on the 18ins gauge tramway, opened in 1904, which ran for nearly one mile to the nearby waterworks. Traffic was subject to tidal conditions which were normally only favour- able on two consecutive days every fortnight. By 1928 the navigation had fallen into decay through silting, and so a Sentinel Steam Waggon operating from Doleham Halt brought coal to the wharf. The tramway closed in 1935 and coal was subsequently transported entirely by road.

61. The Hastings & St Leonards Waterworks, built in 1903, housed two 410hp Tangye triple expansion steam driven engines and, although not in regular use, one is available on stand-by to supplement the Hastings water supply. The tramway was used by an 0-4-0 tank engine which pulled four or five wagons carrying 18 to 20 tons of coal. Traces of the line can still be seen.

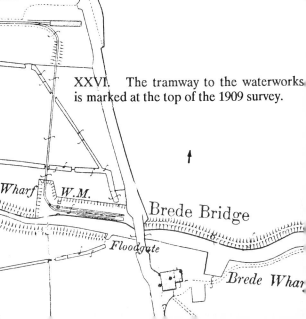

XXVI. The tramway to the waterworks is marked at the top of the 1909 survey.

Wharf W.M.

Brede Bridge

Floodgate

Brede Whar

RIVER TILLINGHAM

The River Tillingham is little more than a stream which rises near Staple Cross and flows ten miles before joining the River Brede at Rye. The tidal reaches had been used for water traffic since the 18th century, and in 1786 a navigational sluice was erected above Strand Quay to prevent the tide flowing up and to improve the scouring of the Strand Channel.

The navigation was used by narrow barges from Rye servicing the farms in the Tillingham Valley. Wharves were established at Ferry Bridge, Leasam Farm, Marshall's Farm and Marley Farm (two miles from Rye), and there may have been occasional traffic further upstream. The main trade was in coal and agricultural produce.

Navigation above Rye ceased in 1928 when the Commissioners of the Levels, the Kent and Sussex County Councils and the Borough of Rye, jointly carried out major improvements to Rye Harbour, which included the replacement of the sluice upstream of Strand Quay by the pinnock which exists today. The river can now only be explored by canoe or portable boat.

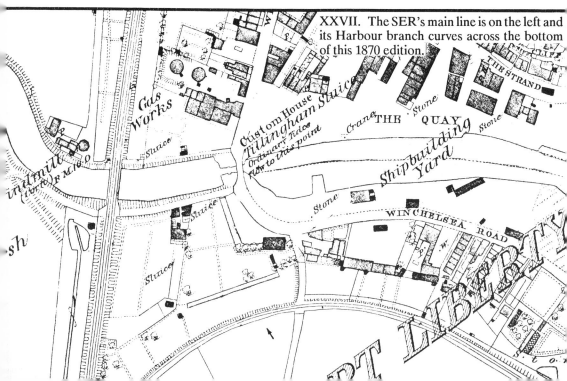

XXVII. The SER's main line is on the left and its Harbour branch curves across the bottom of this 1870 edition.

63. A river barge on the Tillingham at Strand Quay, Rye, in about 1930.

◀━━━━

2. The junction of the Tillingham and Brede vers is illustrated, along with Strand Quay, hich has been in use since about 1480. ranes and a store house were erected there arly in the 16th century. A longer wharf, 00ft long, was built by Rye Corporation in 790, and during the 19th century large store ouses were erected (including a weight and cale warehouse) and two shipyards were built n the opposite bank. Access to the quay eteriorated in the 1930s when importers ound it possible to navigate ships on only six ays out of fourteen due to lack of draught. In 935 both sides of the quay were reconstructed ith steep paling, thereby enabling Thames arges to discharge coal into the bunkers off he Winchelsea Road, or to the Rye Gasworks.

4. This rare picture of the flash lock at the ntrance to Strand Quay was published in 875. The lock permitted barges to pass up he Tillingham to discharge coal for the neigh-ouring farms and collect agricultural pro-uce. The smock windmill on a brick base has stage, four sweeps and a fantail. In 1930 it as burnt down but was rebult in 1932.

ROYAL MILITARY CANAL

The canal was built by Sir John Rennie and Major General John Brown to serve as part of a defence work to Romney Marsh and the Dungeness Peninsular during the Napoleonic Wars. A string of Martello Towers was built along the Kent and Sussex Coast from 1805 to 1808, but since these alone could not have prevented a landing by French troops, and the proposed flooding of the marsh would have taken several days, Prime Minister William Pitt authorised the building of the canal and military road from Sandgate near Hythe, to Cliff End near Winchelsea. Work was begun in October 1804 and the canal filled with water in August 1806. Iden Lock was opened in September 1808. By 1816 the military road, which ran behind the parapet bordering the canal, was reported to be in good condition.

Initially the canal was used by the Royal Waggon Train for moving stores and carrying troops between Winchelsea and Shorncliffe. In 1809 4,740 soldiers passed along the waterway by barge which was opened as a public navigation in April 1810, by which time the threat of invasion had passed.

The total length of the defence work was 28 miles which included over two miles of the Brede Navigation, half a mile of the River Tillingham and three miles of the River Rother. It was never totally finished as the redoubts at Sandgate and Cliff End were not completed, nor were the

65. It is perhaps the historical associations which make the canal so interesting to the visitor. It was in the first place approved and promoted by William Pitt the Younger when Prime Minister and Lord Warden of the Cinque Ports and it was he who kept his eye on it while it was being built as did Sir John Moore, who was at that time commander of the defence force at Shorncliffe and is illustrated here.

cannons ever put in place.

The canal was managed by the Royal Staff Corps, but when this was disbanded in 1837, it was controlled by the Board of Ordnance until 1877, when much of it was leased to the Lords of the Level of Romney Marsh for 999 years at an annual rent of one shilling (5p).

The canal was also used by a regular passage boat service between Hythe, Appledore and Iden Lock until 1833 when it was stopped because of the damage being caused to the banks by the "frequent and rapid transit of the boat". A service was resumed in 1839 and continued until about 1850.

15,000 tons was the most the canal carried in any one year, but this was probably because in the early years tolls were relatively high and commercial traffic was not over encouraged by the military authorities.

The arrival of the railway from London to Ashford in 1842 resulted in a brief, but considerable, upsurge in the carriage of coal and timber from Rye to Bilsington and Bonnington from where they were carted to Ashford station. Traffic reverted to its old level when the railway reached Folkestone and remained fairly constant between 1850 and 1867, when the average trade exceeded 10,000 tons of which hop poles formed an important part.

In 1874 the canal and military road between Winchelsea and Cliff End was sold, and in 1877 the War Department leased the waterway from Iden to West Hythe to the Lords of Romney Marsh, and the remainder to the Corporation of Hythe. It was the arrival of the railway at Hythe in 1874 which took away much of the canal's commercial traffic, and it had ceased altogether to Hythe by 1883, when the West Hythe dam had been constructed in the interests of land drainage. Between 1886 and 1902 the waterway rarely carried over 500 tons and the last barge passed through Iden lock in 1909.

Waterways explorer P. Bonthron wrote in 1916 of his excursion from Rye to Sandgate and remarked "strangely enough in all our many experiences of canal travelling, we had never heard before of this waterway". In spite of Iden

66. The Sussex section of the canal was dug from Winchelsea to Cliff End (3 miles) between 1804 and 1806. It was never used commercially although military barges carried shingle from the wharf at Cliff End for the building of the military road which ran behind the canal's northern parapet. This had been completed by 1810 and when the flood gates between the canal and the Brede at Winchelsea became unserviceable, they were replaced in 1814 by a dam over which the present road is carried. The right flank at Cliff End was protected by Martello Towers 37 and 38 and the canal itself was scarped into the cliff face so that the beach could only be reached by crossing a wooden bridge. This was dismantled in 1817 and replaced by the present embankment, which carried the road to Dymchurch Wall. Both the Martello Towers and the beginning of the canal have now been swept away by the encroaching sea.

←

67. The entrance to the Royal Military Canal from the Rother Navigation at Iden 1971.

Lock not being in use, the need to portage their double-sculling skiff at West Hythe dam and elsewhere, and "a little weed trouble, ... we found the military canal a fine waterway and no pleasanter trip could be undertaken".

The Southern Water Authority now exercise control of the water supply between Iden and West Hythe and, as a result of local government changes, Shepway District Council has been responsible for the eastern end of the canal since 1974.

The Seabrook section of the canal at Hythe was scheduled as an ancient monument in 1986, but unfortunately efforts to save the demolition of the former Royal Staff Corps Barracks in Hythe in 1974 were unsuccessful. The proposal in 1987 to alter the terminal length of canal bed to form part of a new marina will be a pity, but its loss would be mitigated if the developers undertake to restore the redoubt and establish a canal museum. The fact that both banks of this section of the canal have been allowed to become overgrown and unattended is much to be regretted.

8. To the left of the lock are the officer's quarter's. The subaltern posted there in 1810 was also responsible for the Cliff End Section of the canal. The barracks and the officer's quarters at Iden were originally constructed of brick noggin and by the early 1820s were fast going into decay. They were rebuilt by the Royal Staff Corps in stone in 1824 as inscribed above the doorway on the north entrance. After 1838 the building housed the toll collector.

69. This is Iden Barracks, which housed the detachment of soldiers responsible for guarding the defence work. It was also used by the toll collector until the Royal Staff Corps were disbanded in 1838.

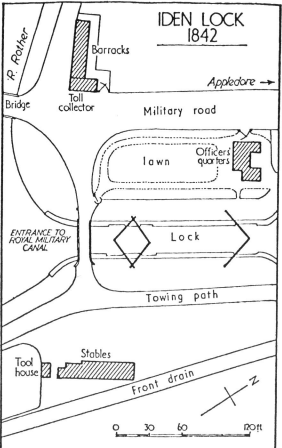

IDEN LOCK 1842

R. Rother

Barracks

Toll collector

Bridge

Appledore →

Military road

Officers quarters

lawn

ENTRANCE TO ROYAL MILITARY CANAL

Lock

Towing path

Tool house

Stables

Front drain

N

0   30   60   120 ft

70. Regular commercial traffic through Iden lock ceased in 1902 although it was not until 1909 that the last barge passed through to Appledore. This 1930 view shows the derelict lock gates but the channel remains clear.

XXVIII. Iden lock opened for navigation in 1808, was equipped with three sets of gates, a conventional pair of mitre gates at the top or canal end, and two pairs at the river end, one pointing in either direction. The extra pair were intended to keep out the river in times of flood or spring tides. Now there is only one pair of lower wooden gates and the upper gates have been replaced by a tilting weir, which does not allow boats to pass.

71. During WWII and the post-war years the lock gates crumbled and the channel became choked and overgrown, as this 1963 photo shows. Not until the late 1960s did the Kent River Board restore the channel to its former condition. By building a dam instead of a lock at Appledore, to raise the water level and to improve land drainage, they erected a further impediment to navigation being restored.

XXIX. Diagram of the layout at Stone in 1810 which was typical of the other locations.

72. This stone, erected in 1806 on the parapet of the military canal, marks the boundary between Kent and Sussex. Whether this was done to commemorate the inspection of the canal by the Commander-in-Chief, the Duke of York and by his brother, the Duke of Cambridge in August 1806 is uncertain. It seems a strange time to erect such a stone, unless it was intended as a gesture to parody the building of the imposing marble pillar begun in Boulogne in 1804 to celebrate the invasion which was never to take place.

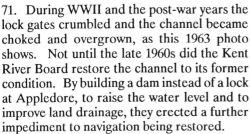

73, 74 and 75 show 1971 views of the existing station houses. These were built by each bridge for the guards primarily to prevent smuggling and superintend the parapet, but also to break the bridges in the event of invasion. Each station could accommodate one NCO and eight men. "They are of course small but sufficient for the purpose" wrote one director. Originally constructed of black noggin, they were rebuilt in stone between 1822 and 1825. After 1840 only eight of the station houses were manned.

The station at Shorncliffe was built over the canal by the sluice just above the surface of the water and this had to be rebuilt on dry land in 1819 as its location had been extremely prejudicial to the health of the soldiers.

When the Royal Staff Corps was disbanded, sappers occupied the station houses, but in 1841 it was agreed that pensioners from the Board of Ordnance should do the job. When the War Office disposed of the canal, some of the station houses were sold while others fell into decay and were demolished. By 1989 only four survived.

76. The building of the canal involved excavating a deep channel around Romney Marsh and using the excavated material to form a high defensive parapet. A unique feature of the canal was the way the banks and parapet were built so that the gun positions could enfilade each length to flank the crossings as illustrated in this aerial view of Ruckinge in 1960. The military road, now a grass grown bridleway, runs behind the parapet.

77. This 1829 view of the ruins of Studfall Castle, a Roman fortress demolished by a landslip, shows the canal below and the line of Martello Towers.

78. The 1807 Act allowed licensed pleasure boats to use the canal. Throughout the waterway's history applications were received for permission to use small sailing boats, birch canoes, four oar galleys and even a wherry with a pair of sculls or a wager boat. In 1853 the Folkestone Rowing Club took a trip in their galley. This photo shows an Edwardian steam pinnace in use.

80. This oil painting of Hythe must have been painted in 1807. The Royal Military canal had been dug and filled with water by 1806 but the Royal Staff Corps Barracks were not begun until 1808. To the right of Hythe Church stands the house that was later occupied by the Director of the Royal Military Canal. The wooden bridge was rebuilt in 1814, with stone quoins for the brick piers.

79. Pleasure boating is seen at Hythe, west of Barrack Wharf and the Romney Road Bridge, in 1970. The terminus of the Romney, Hythe & Dymchurch Railway (opened in 1927) is behind the building. The Corporation of Hythe assumed responsibility for its section of canal in 1877. Boating has generally been very popular at Hythe. In 1905 H. G. Wells observed in Kipps that his protagonist had taken Anne "for a row on the Hythe canal. The sun set in a mighty blaze and left a world warm and very still". The only boating station where boats can now be hired is by Town Bridge. Here I counted 52 skiffs and 10 canoes on one occasion in September 1987. However, neither the Southern Water Authority nor Shepway District Council permit motor boats to use the canal, so that pleasure boating is rarely undertaken along other stretches of the canal.

81.   This Shepherd print of Hythe in 1829 shows The Royal Staff Corps Barracks on the left, with the tree lined canal bank in front of it.   On the sea shore stand two Martello Towers protecting Sutherland Fort.   The Royal Staff Corps was disbanded in 1838 and the barracks remained unoccupied from 1842 until 1853 when the School of Musketry was established to provide troops with instruction in the new Enfield Rifle.   The School of Musketry later became the School of Infantry until it was closed in 1969.   In 1974 the fine buildings were demolished, after a public enquiry, to make way for offices for the South Eastern Electricity Board.   The Royal Waggon Train barracks, stables and gun shed were built of memel timber in 1808 and roofed with Bangor slates, brought by barges from Rye.   The detachment of the wagon train stationed at Hythe between 1808 and 1833 sometimes employed ten or more barges and thirty or so horses for moving troops and stores along the canal.

82.   The Royal Staff Corps Barracks as they appeared in 1971 shortly before their demolition.

83. Various passenger boat services operated between Hythe and Appledore, Iden and Rye between 1810 and 1850. Westall's print of "Hythe from the Canal Bridge" published in 1829 illustrates a small passage boat which would have been towed by two horses, one behind the other, along the tow-path. The canal bridges were of the simplest type being initially built in 1805 with timber abutments due to a shortage of bricks. By 1810 these had been replaced with stone or brick but the wooden decking was retained, as depicted here, so that the bridges could easily be broken in the event of enemy invasion.

84. In 1860, the first Hythe Venetian Fete took place. This has continued in various forms until the present day and is now held biennially. This picture was taken in 1970.

85. The defence of the left flank at Sandgate was completed by excavating the canal under a projecting escarpment to a depth of 22ft. A drawbridge which carried the Hythe - Folkestone road across the cut was removed in 1840. On the left is the uncompleted Redoubt or Battery begun by General Twiss in 1809 (as seen in 1971) which blocked part of the Hythe to Sandgate Road - and was partially dismantled in 1841. Subsequent road improvement schemes and neglect have caused most of the building to vanish. What is left is the south wall, some 15 feet high and 75 feet wide on the north bank of the canal. The east wall is about 110 feet long, 11 feet wide and has a height of 4 to 5 feet. Of the west wall only about 15 feet remain. Beneath the east wall is a covered gallery (which is not at present visible nor accessible), which appears to have formed a passage beneath the battery for transporting stores and ammunition. These ruins require attention as in their present state few people are aware of their historical significance. The wharf (on the right) was originally 40 feet long and used for unloading military stores brought by barge for Shorncliffe Camp. It ceased to be used in the 1840s. A public enquiry was held at Folkestone in 1987 to consider whethher this section of the canal should be developed to form a marina.

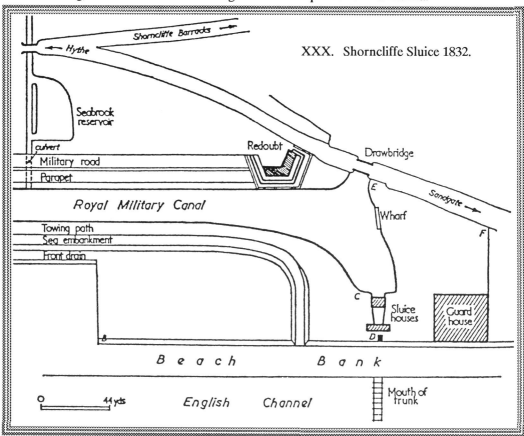

STOUR NAVIGATION

The River Stour rises to the north of Hythe and flows 40 miles to the sea at Pegwell Bay. The 19 miles from the sea to Fordwich are tidal and have always been navigable. An Act of 1515 authorised the improvement of over two miles of the river from Fordwich to Canterbury. Two flash locks at Sturry and Barton were built, but lighters could carry only about 12 tons. In spite of further attempts to keep the navigation open during the 17th century it fell into disrepair and Daniel Defoe, writing in 1724, mentions that coal and timber went up the Stour to Fordwich and then by road to Canterbury. In 1776 the Sandwich Drainage Act authorised the Stonar cut near Richborough, to avoid the river's great meander near Sandwich.

Several plans to improve the navigation during the early 19th century collapsed, although by 1823 the Stour was being used by barges able to carry 30 ton cargoes to Fordwich. In the 1840s considerable consignments of coal and timber were ascending the navigation and at least seven barges were regularly plying between Sandwich and Fordwich bridge. Commercial traffic to Fordwich ceased about 1884.

In 1916 the War Office decided that a new port should be created at Richborough to build barges and ferry military supplies to France. The river was straightened and dredged, new wharves built, a second Stonar cut made. By December the port was operative. A cross channel train ferry called for a turning basin and the enlargement of the river mouth. 140 barges for use on French waterways were completed before the war ended. The port was then used to bring back enormous quantities of war material and salvage. This work completed, the quays and basin at the Sonar Cut fell into dilapidation and ruin. Some commericial traffic continued up the river as far as Sandwich until the 1970s but today only Brett's use the former port of Richborough.

36. Low tide at the junction of the Stonar Cut with the Stour at Richborough presented a sad scene in 1989. The cut is not navigable and the motorised barge, built for use in the Dardanelles, is now used as a house boat. Timberlake's wastepaper business on the left now uses road transport. Oil barges used to operate until some ten years ago but now only Brett's (lower downstream) use the Stour for carrying aggregate and gravel.

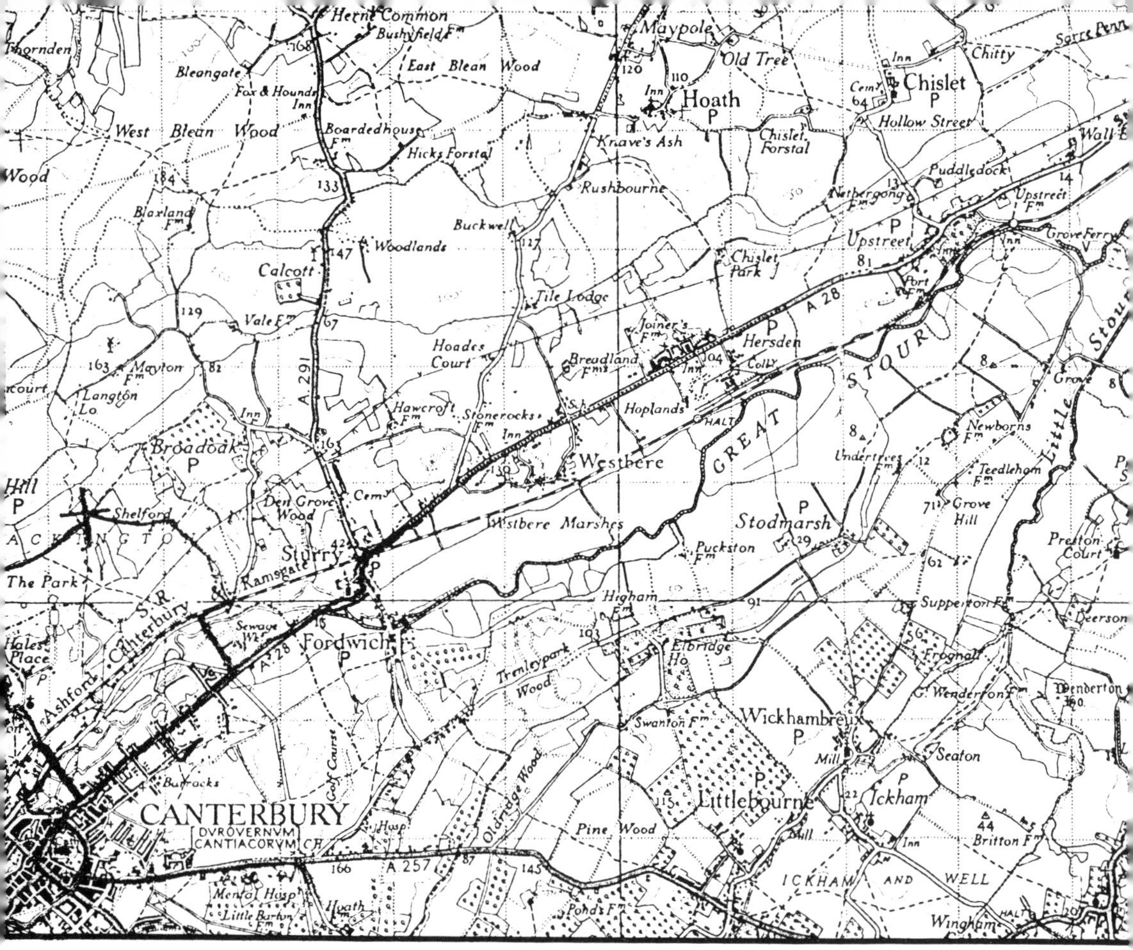

A New Oarsman's Guide, 1896.

Miles			Miles		
	Ashford Bridge -	Stat. S. E. R. (¼ mile). Inn, Kent Arms. The engine and carriage works of the S. E. R. are on the S. side of the town. River narrow and shallow with fair stream.	18½	Fordwich -	The port of Canterbury and formerly a shipping place, but only a few smal sels trade here now. The river w and is tidal below. Inn, George & Dr
2	Willesborough Br.		23¾	Grove Ferry -	Stat. S. E. R.
5¼	Wye Bridge -	Stat. S. E. R. The bridge dates from 1638. At Olantigh below, the river is spanned by a Suspension Bridge with wire netting which blocks the channel. There is however a practicable portage over two weirs and through a small tunnel on a backwater. Many shallows before Chilham.	26¾	Channel to Sarre (and the sea near The Reculvers) -	Left bank. Sarre (1 mile). The s miles). This cut has several sluice and other obstacles, and requires at one long portage.
8	Godmersham Bridge		27⅛	Junction of Little Stour River	Right bank.
10¼	Chilham Bridge -	Stat. S. E. R. Pretty country. Chilham Castle (1616) is a fine ivy-mantled mansion. Portage at Chilham Mill.	29⅛	Red House Ferry -	The river here was once 1 mile wide.
13	Chartham Bridge -	Stat. S. E. R. Difficult portages at the flour-mill and paper-mill.	31¼	Railway Bridge -	Minster Stat. S. E. R. 1¼ mile left bar
14	Milton Bridge		32½	Stonar Cut (300 yds.) - Red Lion Inn	Leads to Pegwell Bay. Was made to re river of flood water and sluice is raised for that purpose. A portage neck of land saves 5 miles.
15¾	Canterbury Bridge	Stats. S. E. and L. C. & D. Rs. Hotels, Fleece, Rose. The Cathedral, St. Martin's Church, West Gate, Dane John Park, Chequers Inn, etc., are the principal sights. The row through the slums is disagreeable. Portage at the mill below.	33¼	Richborough Castle	Right bank (¼ mile). Remains of large Roman works. The walls are 24 ft. high.
18¼	Sturry Bridge -	Stat. S. E. R. (¼ mile) left bank. Portage at the mill (the last on the river).	34½	Sandwich Bridge -	Stat. S. E. R. One of the Cinque F Little trade now owing to harbour h been allowed to silt up ; but in the century was the "most famous of a English harboures." Has many q old buildings. Golfing centre.
			38	Pegwell Bay -	

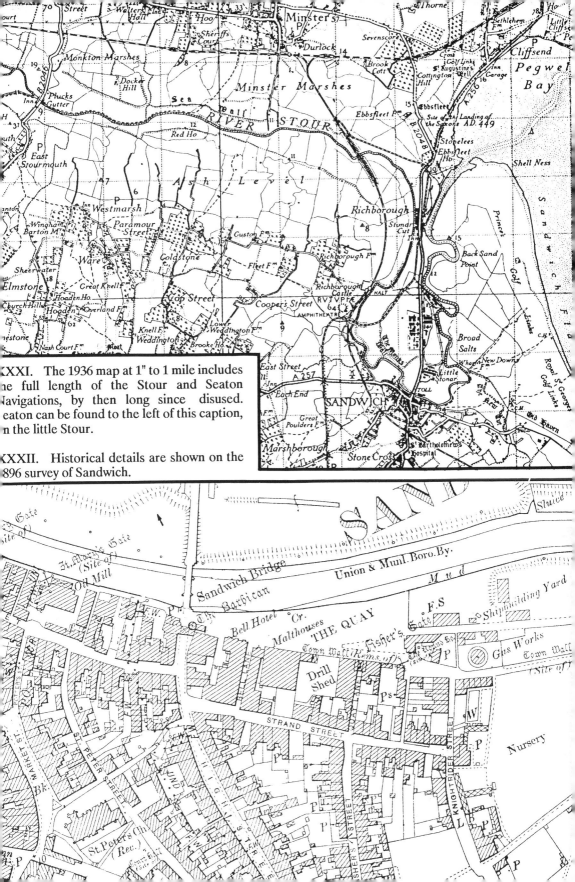

XXXI. The 1936 map at 1" to 1 mile includes the full length of the Stour and Seaton Navigations, by then long since disused. Seaton can be found to the left of this caption, on the little Stour.

XXXII. Historical details are shown on the 1896 survey of Sandwich.

87. The balance bridge at Sandwich was constructed in 1762 and rebuilt in 1795. This view looking downstream, with the Bell Hotel on the right, was drawn in about 1830.

88. A Medway sailing barge moored at the quay below Sandwich bridge was the subject of a postcard posted in May 1919.

89. After regular commercial barge traffic to Fordwich had ceased in the 1880s, Sandwich continued to be a busy port for small coastal traders as this 1905 view of the wharves above the bridge indicates.

90. A similar view was taken in 1920, by which time the wharves were almost deserted.

91. Pleasure boats are seen moored below Fordwich Bridge in the 1920s. Fordwich was the port for Canterbury although attempts were made at various times to make the river navigable to King's Bridge, in the city, and so escape the Fordwich Quay dues. A project early in the 18th century partially succeeded but on several occasions Fordwich men seized the barges as they attempted to pass beneath the bridge. The crane, which still stands on the quayside by the Town Hall, was also used for the ducking stool, used as a punishment for wives who misbehaved.

SEATON NAVIGATION

The Seaton Navigation was made by a miller, Edward Kingsford, who wanted to use barges on the Lesser Stour to bring grain to his mill. The waterway extended six miles from the Stour Navigation above Stourmouth to the hamlet of Seaton in the parish of Ickham.

On 10th February 1801, the Canterbury Press announced that a great number of people had assembled at Seaton to see the first barge launched at the new navigation which was almost finished. Mr Kingsford "provided a plentiful cold collation of roast and boiled beef, roast pork, rabbit pies, bread and cheese, a butt of good strong beer, spirituous liquors etc". Six barges were built to bring Russian wheat and coal from Sandwich.

Kingsford invented a contrivance for dredging the river which consisted of a boat, 12ft wide (which was about the width of the stream) fitted with moveable iron scrapers, which was driven downstream by the force of the current. This machine was used once a year to maintain a draught of about 4ft and took five or six days to remove the mud which was pushed out into the Stour. Although no Parliamentary authority was granted for making the navigation, section 97 of the 1825 Canterbury Navigation Act allowed the owner of "the corn mill, wharf and warehouse" on the Seaton Navigation at Seaton to pay only one half of the river rates for a period of 21 years. Clearly the Seaton Navigation had proved its utility and the clause was inserted to compensate the owner for part of his expenditure.

From Seaton goods were also transferred to wagons for the neighbouring villages and the five mile journey to Canterbury. In favourable conditions there was also some barge traffic to Littlebourne and Wingham by a tributary stream.

It seems that Kingsford's dredging gadget may not have been a total success, for in about 1840 a lock or flood gate was erected near Pluck's Gutter which allowed the Lesser Stour to be navigated to Seaton by barges drawing not more than 3ft 6ins. Traffic ceased in 1860, but barges remained moored at the wharf until at least 1877. In the early 1880s the three storey building became a rubber factory. It is now a private residence.

XXXIII. Seaton Mill is shown as a corn mill on the 1877 and 1898 editions and as a rubber mill on this 1907 survey. The dock and barge turning area has been filled in on the 1937 version. The navigation is on the right.

92. Seaton Mill seen in this eastward view as it appeared in about 1890 when it was a rubber factory. The head of water visible here was provided for the mill.

93. The site of the wharf and dock as it appears in 1989. This was situated on the opposite side of the mill depicted in the previous picture.

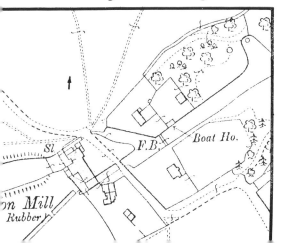

MEDWAY NAVIGATION

The River Medway is Kent's most important river. It rises near the borders of Surrey and Sussex and reaches the North Sea after flowing 70 miles. The lower tidal reaches up to Maidstone had, like the Thames, been used by craft from time immemorial, and as early as the 16th century attempts had been made to make the river navigable above Maidstone. The removal of fish weirs, fallen trees and other obstructions enabled small boats to reach Yalding, six miles above Maidstone, by about 1580. However, the Commissioners of Sewers were more concerned with the free flow of the river than with its navigation. While the ironmasters and timber growers of the Weald needed water transport, the riparian and mill owners claimed the river was private property and were uncooperative. Further attempts in the 17th century were frustrated although in 1665 the ironmasters obtained an Act to make the river navigable for the carriage of ordnance and other products of the Weald.

Again no action followed, and it was not until 1740 that a second Act was passed, which authorised the river to be made navigable to Forest Row, three miles south-east of East Grinstead and 15 miles above Tonbridge. The principal object was the carriage of timber for the Navy, since the cost of carrying it by land was excessive. Fourteen locks werre built to take barges of about 40 tons and the work was completed to Tonbridge in 1741. The trade in timber, iron and coal was so successful that by 1767 a good dividend could be declared. So began a run of continuous

XXXIV.   The 1930 survey at a quarter of an inch to one mile includes the River Medway between Sheerness, Rochester, Maidstone and Tonbridge.

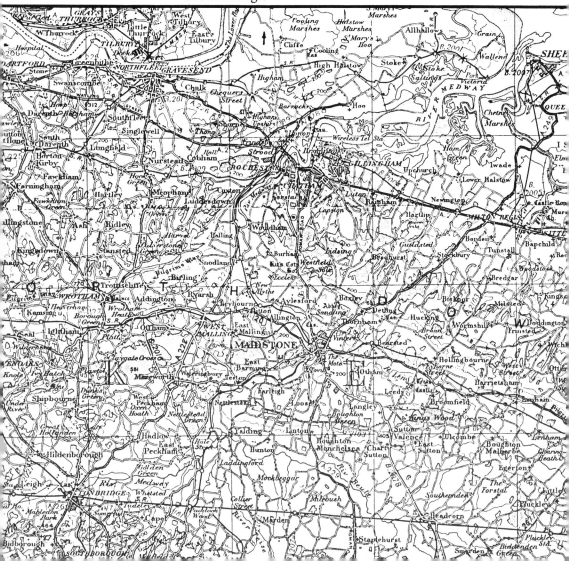

dividends which was to last until 1869.

The Medway below Maidstone remained tidal until the Act of 1792 empowered the improvement of the river from Aylesford to Maidstone. In 1798 Hasted, the Kent historian, described the river at Maidstone as carrying a considerable traffic to Rochester, Chatham and London. A further Act of 1802 authorised the rebuilding of Aylesford Bridge which was a hinderance to navigation and allowed Allington tidal lock to be built. This enabled craft to reach Maidstone at all states of the tide. Not, however, until 1825 were the two arches of Allington Bridge removed and a larger arch subsituted.

In 1807 the Upper Medway Navigation Company announced that they had fitted up a barge to carry shop goods, ironmongery and goods in general from Maidstone to Tonbridge and places between. It loaded every Monday.

Traffic, which in 1822 amounted to 16,000 tons, had increased to 32,000 in 1830 and 50,000 in 1835.

The arrival of the railway from Maidstone to Tonbridge in 1844 goaded the company into building a tramroad between Tonbridge Wharf and the station, and establishing coal wharves at neighbouring villages like Edenbridge and Penshurst. Difficulties arose with the South Eastern Railway however, and in spite of toll reductions, traffic began to gradually decline. In 1868 Branbridges Mill at East Peckham closed. In 1888 the profit was only £127 from a revenue of £2,414.

In 1880, Allington Lock was enlarged which enabled Maidstone College Lock to be removed. The collapse of East Farleigh Lock in 1909 closed the upper navigation for three months, and the resultant loss of traffic opened the way for the Upper Medway Navigation & Consevancy Act (1911) to be passed. The Conservancy replaced 13 locks by 10 larger ones and ensured a navigable draught of seven feet. Navigation was fully restored to Tonbridge in September 1915. Traffic declined further after the end of WWI and the last toll paying barge reached Tonbridge in 1927, Yalding in 1928 and Tovil in 1977.

In 1934 the Conservancy was superseded by the River Medway Catchment Board and later by the Southern Water Authority who maintain the navigation from Allington Lock to the concrete footbridge below the flood barrier at Leigh. Below Allington Lock the tidal length of the river is controlled by the Medway Ports Authority.

MEDWAY (LOWER)
NAVIGATION

94. Upnor Castle, depicted here in 1830, was built in 1561 to defend Chatham Dockyard. When, however, the Dutch sailed up the Medway in 1667, it could do no more than fire its guns. The village lies one mile downstream from Rochester and 13 miles from the Medway's estuary at Sheerness.

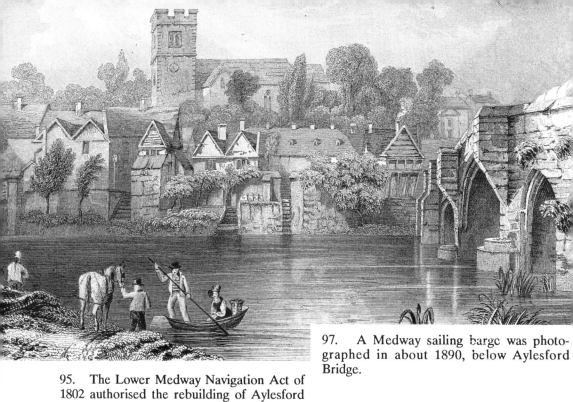

97.   A Medway sailing barge was photographed in about 1890, below Aylesford Bridge.

95.   The Lower Medway Navigation Act of 1802 authorised the rebuilding of Aylesford Bridge, one of the five Tudor bridges over the river.   It was a hindrance to navigation although this is not readily evident from this downstream 1793 drawing.

96.   Aylesford Bridge and church is seen in 1830.   The 14th century bridge has six small pointed arches and a wider central navigation arch, through which barges passed with lowered masts.

98.   Until 1792 the river was tidal to Maidstone. Allington Lock was then built as a flash lock to enable barges to reach the town on all states of the tide. This view was drawn in 1830. In the late 1840s the single gate was replaced by a pound lock with a double set of gates.

99.   Maidstone has been an important inland port since the 16th century. The chief trade in the early part of the 18th century was making linen thread, planting hops and grinding corn for the Navy.   The steam tug *Ranger* waits in Allington Lock in about 1926, with *Verona* at its stern and *Three Brothers* alongside.

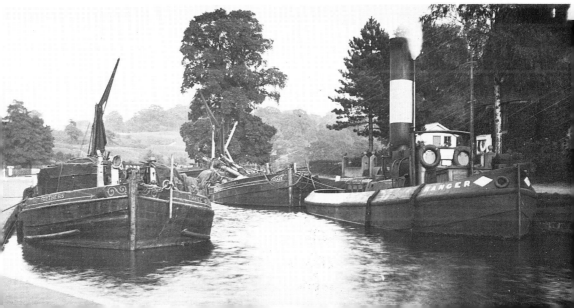

100. Maidstone Bridge was depicted by
Westall in 1829, looking downstream. The
bridge was demolished shortly after the
adjacent three span bridge had been
opened in 1879. The Upper Medway Navigation Company was flourishing with twice
weekly company barges running   between
Tonbridge and London. Hops were an
important downstream cargo and barley, oats,
wheat, peas, malt, linseed and shop goods
were the main upstream traffic. Independent carriers offered a daily service during
the hop season.

UPPER MEDWAY NAVIGATION

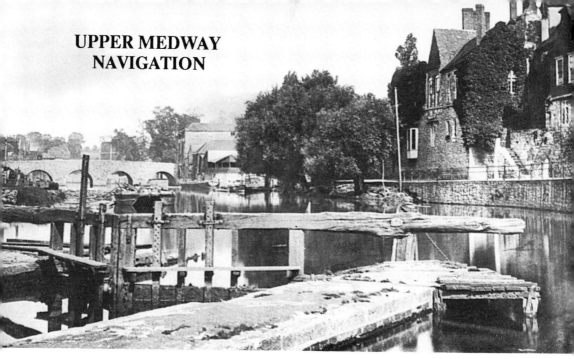

101. The original boundary with the Lower Medway was below Maidstone Bridge, near Faith Street, but in 1907 this was changed to a point about 300 yards above the bridge. A little upstream of Maidstone Bridge was College Lock, the first lock on the upper Medway Navigation. In 1880, the Lower Medway Navigation Company deepened Allington Lock, raising the water levels. As College Lock had been partially washed away by floods that year, the alterations at Allington meant that it could be removed in 1881. The paddles on College Lock were identical to those that were found until recently at Worsfold Gates on the Wey Navigation.

102. East Farleigh Bridge and Lock as depicted in 1790. Its ancient bridge of five arches and massive cutwaters dates from the 15th century. One of the arches (not visible) has been altered to allow for the towpath.

103. This is Farleigh Bridge, lock and weir, as it appeared in 1830.

104. In the winter of 1909-10 East Farleigh Lock collapsed and finally caused the end of the Upper Medway Navigation Company, which was in financial straits. The river was closed for three months, until a bill was promoted in Parliament to transfer its control to an independent Conservancy under Kent County Council. The Conservancy took control of the river in June 1911, closing the lower part until 1913, and the upper section to Tonbridge until 1915. The photograph shows the lock in about 1890 with a barge leaving it on its way downstream to Maidstone.

105. Branbridges Mill at East Peckham is seen here as it appeared in 1790. The bridge was a strange structure with one small arch, a massive cut-water and a wide unarched opening spanned by some form of timber construction. Either the original arch had fallen or else the platform was intended to be lifted or swung to allow barges to pass. The mill closed in 1868, and the bridge was entirely reconstructed in 1906. The lock formerly sited downstream of Branbridges was one of the three eliminated during the reconstruction that was completed in 1915. Barge traffic continued to Branbridges until 1928.

106. Great Bridge at Tonbridge was 104 feet in length and had five arches in the 16th century. In 1775-76 the dilapidated structure was demolished and a new bridge of three arches took its place, as depicted here in 1790. In 1837 the local guide book stated "Immediately below Great Bridge is a spacious wharf for the accommodation of the trade on the river which is now very considerable".

107. In this 1896 view of Tonbridge, pleasure boats can be seen available for hire. The Great Bridge was rebuilt in the 18th century and again in 1887, when iron railings were substituted for the stone parapet.

108. In this 1970 aerial photograph the site of Wise's Tunbridge Ware Factory was to the right of the Great Bridge. The building was pulled down in 1886 and rebuilt in 1888. Tonbridge Castle is in the background and the New Wharf at the bottom left.

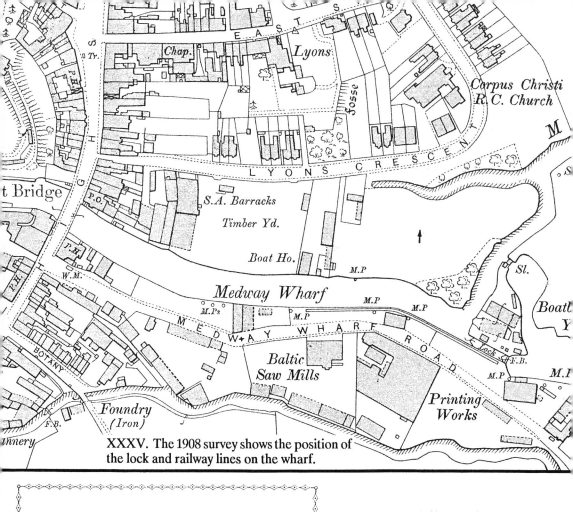

XXXV. The 1908 survey shows the position of the lock and railway lines on the wharf.

The straight mile, one mile west of Tonbridge was sketched by David Maxwell in 1920.

PROPOSED PENSHURST CANAL

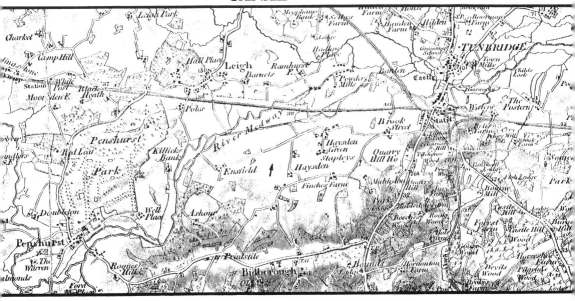

XXXVI. The 1874 revision at 1" to 1 mile shows the three cuts made near the river between Tonbridge and Penshurst, in the period 1829 and 1831.

109. The Straight Mile has been bridged by the recent Tonbridge Bypass (the A21) and halved by the creation of Hayesden Reservoir. In 1989, the remainder was preserved as a bridle-path, but was much overgrown.

The Upper Medway Navigation Act of 1740 authorised the river to be made navigable to Forest Row, 15 miles above Tonbridge, but scarcity of water, doubts about the probable traffic and the number of watermills appears to have deterred the company from carrying out the work. However in 1828 Mr James Christie purchased Tonbridge Mill, and formed the Penshurst Canal Company to extend the navigation six miles from Tonbridge, under the power of the Upper Medway's Act, which allowed others to do so if the company itself did not. Cutting began in March 1829 and the first stone of the lower of two locks was laid in May 1830. Joseph Priestley writing in 1831 stated that it was "in consequence of the recent discovery of a very valuable quarry of building stone on the south side of the river near Penshurst which prompted the extension". His inference that the work had been completed was incorrect. Although three cuts were made, only the section above Barden, "the Long Reach", was completed. The continuation known as the "Straight Mile" was never filled with water. A notice in the Maidstone Journal on 3rd April 1832 offered land for sale at Haysden which included "part of the navigable canal from Tonbridge to Penshurst" and prospective bargees were told they would have "command" over the canal. Although a Parliamentary Bill was introduced in both 1834 and 1836, which included clauses to extend the navigation to Forest Row, the Medway Navigation never proceeded beyond the gunpowder mills at Leigh.

In 1920 author Donald Maxwell explored the river above Tonbridge in a motor-boat, noted the single pair of lock gates at the entrance of the cut leading to the powder mills and its use by a ballast lighter.

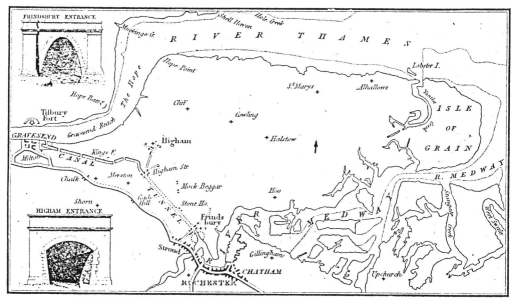

111. Barges and a schooner stand in Strood Dock in 1904. The schooner is discharging coal.

The canal linked the Thames, at Gravesend, with the Medway, at Frindsbury. It was seven miles long and had two locks. Craft using the canal were saved the 47 mile passage round the Isle of Grain.

The initial Act was passed in 1800 but two further Acts were required before the canal was opened on 14th October 1824. Its main feature was Higham Tunnel, 3946 yards long, which was the second longest canal tunnel built in Britain, being exceeded in length only by Stanedge Tunnel, on the Huddersfield Narrow Canal, which is 5415 yards. Higham, however, was a wide tunnel (over 26 feet) with a towpath, whereas Stanedge was only 7ft 1ins, with no towpath.

The majority of craft using the canal were sailing barges which were unable to pass each other in the tunnel, and as trade picked up the congestion forced the company to close the canal for ten weeks, during early 1830, in order to build a passing place. The tunnel was opened out for about 200ft at the point where the valley above was nearest to the tunnel arch, producing a 100ft deep rock sided cutting with a small basin.

◄────────

XXXVII. A plan of the Thames & Medway Canal at 3" to 1 mile at the time of its opening in 1824.

◄────────

110. This is a northward view of the entrance to Frindsbury Basin (Strood) and the canal from the Medway in 1980. The dock was closed in 1962 and the whole site has been levelled, except for the outer entrance lock gates. The tunnel in the background is still used by the railway.

The main items carried were agricultural products, beer, cement and groceries. There was some passenger traffic, but early steamboats had to be taken off as they damaged the banks. Despite a steady trade, the canal was never a financial success, and in February 1844, the company decided to build a single track railway alongside the canal as far as Higham and then through the tunnel. One rail was on the towing path and the other was supported on timbers above the water. The Thames and Medway Canal and the Gravesend and Rochester Railway continued in co-existence for 18 months, when both were sold to the South Eastern Railway. The company soon filled in the canal from Higham to Frindsbury, opening a double track line through the tunnel on 23 August 1847.

The remainder of the waterway was renamed the Gravesend & Rochester Canal and was used by local farmers to carry down produce for the ships off Gravesend and bring back manure for the hop fields. When the hop fields around Higham were put to other uses in the early 1920s barge traffic ceased. In 1934 the Southern Railway obtained an Abandonment Act. In 1970 planning consent was granted to infill the section between Gravesend Basin and Denton and this land is now used for light industry. The rest of the canal bed is (1989) filled with reeds and the occasional pool of water.

The Thames & Medway Canal Association was formed in 1976 to campaign for the reopening of as much of the canal as is feasible, and has indeed organised working parties to remove reed beds and rubbish.

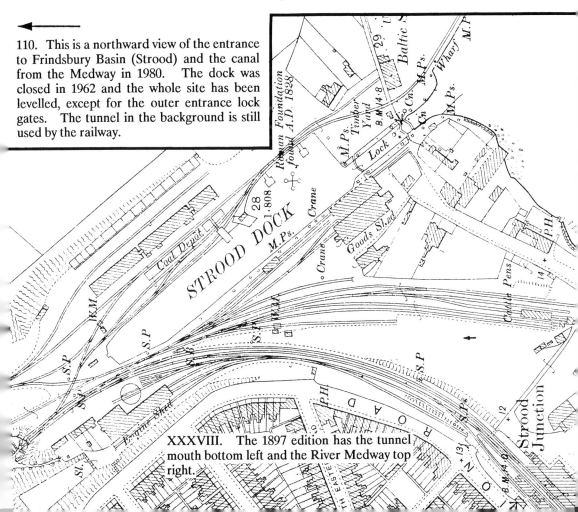

XXXVIII. The 1897 edition has the tunnel mouth bottom left and the River Medway top right.

1825.

THAMES AND MEDWAY CANAL.

RATES OF TONNAGE.

SPECIES OF GOODS.	Per Ton. Per Mile.	Whole Length of Canal.	SPECIES OF GOODS.	Per Ton. Per Mile.	Whole Length of Canal.
Freestone..........	.. 1d. ..	5d. per Ton.	Flour	.. 2d. ..	1s 2d per Ton.
Limestone	.. 1d. ..	5d. ditto.	Wheat............	.. 2d. ..	1s 2d ditto
Chalk............	.. 1d. ..	5d. ditto.	Barley............	.. 2d. ..	1s 2d ditto
Bricks............	.. 1d. ..	5d. ditto.	Oats	.. 2d. ..	1s 2d ditto
Tiles..............	.. 1d. ..	5d. ditto.	Beans............	.. 2d. ..	1s 2d ditto
Slates............	.. 1d. ..	5d. ditto.	Peas	.. 2d. ..	1s 2d ditto
Sand	.. 1d. ..	5d. ditto.	Malt............	.. 2d. ..	1s 2d ditto
Stones............	.. 1d. ..	5d. ditto.	Corn in the Straw .	.. 2d. ..	1s 2d ditto
Clay....	.. 1d. ..	5d. ditto.	Hay	.. 2d. ..	1s 2d ditto
Dung............	.. 1d. ..	5d. ditto.	Straw	.. 2d. ..	1s 2d ditto
Manure	.. 1d. ..	5d. ditto.	Faggots	.. 2d. ..	1s 2d ditto
Tin..	.. 1d. ..	5d. ditto.			
Iron Stone.	.. 1d. ..	5d. ditto.			
Pig Iron..	.. 1d. ..	5d. ditto.	Fruit............	.. 3d. ..	1s 9d per Ton.
Pig Lead	.. 1d. ..	5d. ditto.	Coke	.. 3d. ..	1s 9d ditto
Lime	.. 1d. ..	7d. ditto.	Timber, rough	.. 3d. ..	1s 9d ditto
			Hemp............	.. 3d. ..	1s 9d ditto
			Bark............	.. 3d. ..	1s 9d ditto
Cattle	.. 2d. ..	1s. per Ton.	Coals	.. 3d. ..	1s 9d ditto
Potatoes..... ...	.. 2d. ..	1s. ditto.	Culm	.. 3d. ..	1s 9d ditto
Goods	.. 2d. ..	1s. ditto.			
Wares	.. 2d. ..	1s. ditto.	Hops............	.. 6d. ..	2s 6d per Ton.
Merchandize......	.. 2d. ..	1s. ditto.	Wool............	.. 6d. ..	2s 6d ditto

N. B. If Landed or Shipped from the Company's Premises, 2d. per Ton for Wharfage, extra.

Vessels not exceeding 18 feet in breadth and 100 feet in length, and drawing not more than 5 feet water, may pass along the whole line of the Canal.

An empty return Barge or Vessel, having passed the Canal loaded.......Nil.

An empty Barge or Vessel, going for and returning with Lading ....Nil.

An empty Barge or Vessel passing, to be considered as 20 Tuns, at 6d. per Ton, 10s.—and such empty Barge or Vessel returning without Lading within 24 hours, Nil.

112. A train emerges from the west end of the tunnel into Higham station.

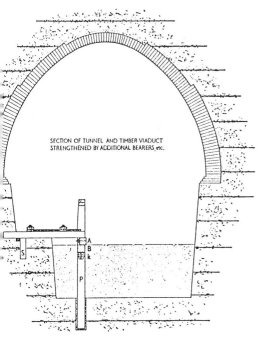

SECTION OF TUNNEL AND TIMBER VIADUCT
STRENGTHENED BY ADDITIONAL BEARERS, etc.

ELEVATION OF IMPROVED VIADUCT

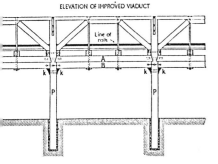

The design of the staging that carried the outer rails of the Gravesend and Rochester Railway through Strood and Higham tunnels.

113.   Soon after the canal was opened, it was found that because of the necessity of having to enter or leave the canal at high tide, vessels often arrived at the canal entrance together.   This resulted in such a delay to boats passing through the tunnel that any time saved in taking the canal rather than the coastal route was lost.   It was, therefore, necessary in 1830 to build, in addition to the passing place at Higham, a second passing place in the central portion of the tunnel.

114.   The Thames & Medway Canal, being designed for use by sailing barges, lift or swing bridges were provided.   This one spanned the canal in 1900, near the Gravesend Basin.

115. This cottage stood at the eastern end of the canal basin until 1942. It is seen here in about 1920, the roof having been formed from an upturned hull of a boat, with a window in one side. It was known as Peggoty's house being thought to have inspired Charles Dickens' description in "David Copperfield". At the turn of the century pleasure boats could be hired from here.

116. An aerial view shows Gravesend canal basin and sea lock in 1956. The canal enters the River Thames through the lock (above centre) having passed under the swing bridge (centre right) from Higham. The canal basin has been reduced in size and was bought by Gravesend Borough Council in 1970. It is now maintained for pleasure craft. The canal above the swing bridge was filled in as far as Denton in the 1970s, and is now used by timber merchants and light industry.

DARTFORD & CRAYFORD NAVIGATION

In the early 19th century the River Darent (known as Dartford Creek) was over three miles long, and was a winding tidal channel which could be used up to the wharves at Dartford and Crayford on spring tides by barges carrying 50 tons. At other times, craft had to anchor at Hibbert's Wharf, about a quarter of a mile below the head of navigation which was at Phoenix Mills, and tranship their cargoes into punts carrying around 10 tons.

Plans for a small ship canal to Dartford in 1835 came to nothing, but an Act of 1840 empowered commissioners to improve the navigation and levy tolls. The channel was dredged and a new cut made by 1844. In 1895 a lock was completed just below Dartford to create a floating basin, and at its peak some 200,000 tons were carried per annum. The closure of the London Docks, and in particular the London Paper Mills in 1968, resulted in the navigation becoming totally disused by 1987.

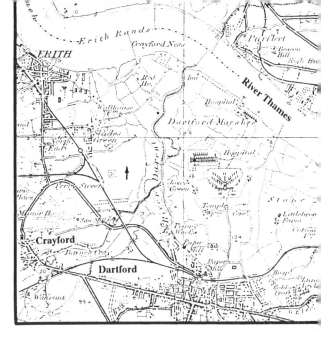

XXXIX. The River Thames is at the top of this 1920 map, shown at 1" to 1 mile, and the navigable length of the River Darent is shown in full.

117. Barges lie at Wellcome's Coal Wharf in about 1930.

118. Here we look south in 1894, past Willow Cottage, towards the first lock, visible in the background. It was designed so that the creek could remain tidal.

Further Reading:

The Kentish Stour 1953 - R. H. Goodsall
A Maritime History of Rye 1978 - J. Collard
The Medway and its Tributaries 1955 - R. H. Goodsall
The Royal Military Canal 1972 - P. A. L. Vine
Sussex River (The Ouse) 1979 - E & N. J. McCarthy
West Sussex Waterways 1985 - P. A. L. Vine

119. Farningham Lees Swing Bridge, at Dartford Creek, in 1910, with corn merchants R & H Strickland's warehouse in the centre. Dartford Lock is at the right of the centre.